THE SCREEN TRAVELER'S GUIDE

Dedicated to our "map man" Cas, who was never able to see this book printed, but who worked tirelessly on it, and countless others. You gave 23 years and thousands of maps to our books. We will miss you deeply.

THE SCREEN TRAVELER'S GUIDE

CONTENTS

INTRODUCTION

Taking a trip to the movies or settling into a great box set has always been a treat. But there's something even better: seeing where it all takes place in real life.

How often have you watched a scene unfold on-screen and rushed to research where it was filmed, utterly beguiled by its gorgeous setting? That's what's so great about flicks and features—they have the power to not only entertain, shock and provoke thought but also to inspire.

As any cinephile will attest, movies and TV shows have the ability to transport us to places beyond our wildest dreams. Through them, we can escape to the icy plains beyond The Wall, the picture-perfect interior of the Grand Budapest Hotel, and the magical elven forests of Lothlórien. Incredible locations exist on-screen, but in real life? Well, we can get pretty close.

While studios play a significant role in moviemaking, so too does Earth's spectacular scenery. We can't exactly go to Arrakis, per se, but we can roam the deserts where the sci-fi epic *Dune* was shot. And though Hogwarts doesn't exist in real life, we Muggles can still visit the grand castles and cathedrals that made up Harry Potter's school.

If following in the footsteps of your favorite characters sounds like your ideal vacation, then look no further. *The Screen Traveler's Guide* takes a deep dive into the locations (some beautiful, others appealing in their familiarity) that backdrop some of the world's most popular movies and TV shows.

Researched and compiled by a team of self-proclaimed superfans and travel experts, this book is jam-packed with fandom favorites and much-loved classics. But narrowing down the list wasn't easy. For every Potter fan among us, there's a Trekkie; for every Fanpire, a Whovian. Needless to say, fierce debates over what to include ensued.

And they didn't stop there. *The Screen Traveler's Guide* is organized by genre, and just as everyone has their favorite movies and TV shows, we all have our opinions on what constitutes a horror or a family classic. For some of the team, *Jaws* conjures pure terror, but for others, it's a family favorite (someone even argued it could be a murder mystery). Meanwhile, *Blade Runner* sits on a knife edge between crime thriller, action classic, and sci-fi phenomenon. When it comes to it, genres will always be subjective. Fortunately, though, there was one thing we could all agree on: locations are everything.

Some of the sites featured in this book are already very much on the tourist trail, while others will take you way off the beaten path. And even if you can't venture into Mexico's humid jungles in search of the Predator or race around New Zealand's mountains like Frodo and the Fellowship, you can still travel vicariously through these pages. There's no knowing where you might be swept off to.

1

1. Dubrovnik, a key filming location for *Game of Thrones*

2. A production crew behind the scenes

3. Gloucester cathedral, which stood in for Hogwarts

4. *Robin Hood* on location in Wales

2

3

4

PLEASE
BE SILENT
BEHIND CAMERA

Von Sternberg

Director Josef von Sternberg and his crew on set at MGM's studio in 1926

Movies and TV shows have been transporting us to places beyond our wildest imaginations since the dawn of cinema. Real-life locations have long been integral to capturing that magic on-screen—and they're still as important as ever.

ON LOCATION

In 1888, French artist and film pioneer Louis Le Prince recorded 1.66 seconds of his friends walking around a garden in Leeds, in the UK. It's widely believed to be the oldest surviving movie footage in the world, and proof that shooting on location is as old as the motion picture itself.

The early days

Location shooting was once essential. When filmmaking was in its infancy, sophisticated artificial lighting simply wasn't available; filming outside was therefore a way of achieving the right kind of lighting conditions. But as the medium developed in the early 20th century, and technological advances with it, it quickly gave rise to a new phenomenon: the movie studio.

America's original movie capital was in New Jersey, where inventor Thomas Edison built the world's first production studio, the Black Maria, in 1892. Edison was so eager to protect his patents on the new technology, however, that many pioneers of early cinema moved away from the East Coast to escape his

The Black Maria, the world's first motion picture studio, erected in New Jersey

monopoly. Luckily, it didn't take long for them to find the perfect place to establish their movie industry.

Southern California's year-round sunshine (and therefore plenty of natural light) was one of the main reasons why many of America's early movie studios were eager to set up operations in Hollywood, a neighborhood in Los Angeles. But the region had other significant advantages. Given the size and cumbersome nature of early camera equipment, when location shots were needed, it helped to stay within the vicinity of the studio. "Around

MOMENTS IN TIME

1916

Hugely influential documentary and propaganda movie *The Battle of the Somme* takes cameras into the World War I trenches.

Los Angeles you have lakes, coast, hills and deserts, and pretty much every major kind of weather and landscape you might need," explains movie writer Ian Haydn Smith. For moviemakers, recreating distant lands just a stone's throw from the studio was a very real and very enticing prospect.

In the era of silent movies (which ran from the dawn of cinema to the late 1920s), location shooting was common—and not just in Hollywood. On the other side of the Atlantic, for

PEOPLE NOW WENT TO THE CINEMA TO FIND OUT WHAT WAS HAPPENING IN THE WORLD

example, director Sergei Eisenstein was making his mark, marshaling hundreds of extras in Ukraine for the much-imitated Odessa Steps sequence in *Battleship Potemkin* (1925).

But change was coming to Hollywood, and when Al Jolson became the first person to utter words on-screen in

1927's *The Jazz Singer*, it ushered in a whole new age of "talkies." Getting out of the studio was about to get a lot more complicated. The fact that these early cameras were extremely noisy had never been much of a problem for silent movies, but it suddenly became necessary to shut them away in bulky and immobile soundproof cabinets. The microphones of the time also struggled to isolate sounds, making the easy-to-control environment of the studio a more attractive proposition.

Filmmaking gear would gradually become more portable, something accelerated by World War II. "People now expected to go to the cinema to find out what was happening in the world," Smith explains. In order to document the world's events in real time, it became essential to develop smaller cameras that could capture

The Potemkin Stairs in Odessa, Ukraine, as seen in *Battleship Potemkin*

1933

King Kong helps turn the Empire State Building into a legendary movie location.

1939

Director John Ford starts his long-running love affair with Monument Valley in his movie *Stagecoach*.

footage in a range of global conflict zones. And this facilitated new methods of location filmmaking.

Era of change

One of the primary practitioners of these new techniques was the seminal Western movie director John Ford. He may have made 14 movies with John Wayne, but the director's relationship with the epic vistas of the American West was arguably more important to the history of cinema. Across movies like *Stagecoach* (1939), *She Wore a Yellow Ribbon* (1949), and *The Searchers* (1956), Ford repeatedly used Monument Valley *(p134)*—located in the Navajo Nation, between Utah and Arizona—to create stunning backdrops for his stories. The filmmaker's tips on using the horizon were so formative for the young Steven Spielberg that he recreated a meeting with Ford in his semi-autobiographical *The Fabelmans* (2022).

A later, unintentional game changer was the Arthurian musical *Camelot* in 1967. The movie's artificial-looking sets were cited as one of the main reasons for its altogether disappointing box office performance and prompted the industry to prioritize keeping things real going forward.

Location shooting went through a further renaissance in the 1970s, with a new generation of American auteurs using stunning real-life landscapes to

THE LOCATION MANAGER

A location manager is one of the first members of the crew to join a movie or TV production. From the beginning, they'll review the script to decide which scenes will work best in a studio and which will work best on location. The location manager's responsibilities then include finding suitable places to shoot, arranging any necessary permissions to film there, and ensuring cast, crew, and equipment can get in and out safely and efficiently. They frequently collaborate with the director and the production designer.

spectacular effect on genre-defining classics such as *Badlands* (1973) and *Apocalypse Now* (1979). "The reason many of the films from the 1970s worked so well is that they capture a real sense of place," explains Smith. "*Chinatown* (1974), for example, is mesmerizing to watch and part of that is the story, but the other thing that draws you in is the incredible Los Angeles locations."

Modern methods

While many small and medium-size productions will shoot predominantly on location today (it's often far cheaper than building sets in a movie studio), major Hollywood movies and TV shows tend to adopt a more mix-and-match approach. Location manager David Powell explains the factors involved in the decision: "Largely it's based on what a location has to offer and what the script needs. For example, if the filmmakers are looking to film a heavy dialogue scene in a small interior, they'll build that on stage,

1953

Future Ben-Hur director William Wyler creates the ultimate tourist ad for Rome, shooting *Roman Holiday* on location in Italy.

1962

Ursula Andress's Honey Ryder steps out of the sea at Jamaica's Ocho Rios, dispatching James Bond on decades of adventures.

because you'll have complete control [of the environment] there." If the movie instead requires a grand vista or an impressive landscape, it will generally try to shoot on location.

Even when a production has made the decision to venture out into the real world, it's never quite as straight-forward as turning up at a site and letting the cameras roll. "A location manager needs to be able to walk in and see whether somewhere is feasible to be shot in," says Powell. Though today's gear is considerably less bulky than in the early days of film, it can still present the crew with a significant challenge. "Any production comes with

a huge amount of equipment and many cast and crew. It's all well and good finding the perfect lake at the top of a mountain but it's going to cost a lot of money to get everything up there." When transporting equipment seems impossible, there's the tempting option of using VFX to create the image of a mountainous background.

THE PRODUCTION WILL END UP DOING WHAT'S MOST EFFICIENT AND MOST CREATIVE

The production team and location manager will need to weigh the logistics alongside the specific demands of the script. Powell adds: "Production might say, 'This [location] is a lot easier logistically and a lot cheaper,' but if you've got a renowned director on board who says, 'I want that one!' then the film will no doubt go to that chosen location. Essentially the production will end up doing what's most efficient and most creative."

Few movies highlight the trials and tribulations of location shooting quite

Shooting war epic *Apocalypse Now* in south Vietnam

1967

The disappointing box office performance of *Camelot* is partially blamed on its unconvincing studio backdrops.

1968

Steve McQueen and director Peter Yates invent the modern car chase on the streets of San Francisco in *Bullitt*.

like Werner Herzog's controversial *Fitzcarraldo* (1982). The movie documents an opera-loving Irishman's attempt to transport a 320-ton steamship over dry Peruvian land. Herzog wasn't content to fake it; the crew really did lug the vessel over a hill, contending with punishing weather, furious leading actors, and venomous snakes in the process. Multiple crew members died carrying out Herzog's vision, and the movie is a visceral reminder that shooting on location, without the safety of studio conditions, requires care and respect for both cast and environment.

For all the challenges that location shooting can throw up, it remains an essential part of a good filmmaker's arsenal. "Sometimes shooting in a studio just does not compare to the real thing," Powell explains. "You can be effective in a studio, sure, but when you go somewhere and you're looking at this incredible mountainous landscape or surrounded by all this impressive architecture in a city … being there and getting that shot for real is worth its weight in gold." And with such beautiful locations, an entire tourist industry has been born around noteworthy settings.

Screen tourism
When a movie or TV show finds the perfect filming location, it can become as iconic as the stars or the dialogue. It's no surprise, then, that many fans are

A CGI MAKEOVER

Movie locations have often been given a significant CGI makeover by the time they make it to the screen. Sometimes those digital augmentations are obvious—when London's Millennium Bridge was featured in Marvel's *Guardians of the Galaxy* (2014), for example, St. Paul's Cathedral and the famous Thames River skyline were replaced with futuristic architecture from the planet Xandar. Other changes are more subtle. In fact, you'd need to be pretty familiar with Thailand's Maya Bay to spot that Danny Boyle's *The Beach* (2000) added a few extra hills to make the eponymous beach seem even more secluded.

Werner Herzog directing crew on the set of *Fitzcarraldo*

1977
George Lucas uses Tunisian locations to create landscapes from a galaxy far, far away in the original *Star Wars*.

1984
An ordinary New York fire station becomes a superstar when Hook & Ladder 8 Firehouse in Tribeca is chosen to play Ghostbusters HQ.

Paul Hogan on location in Australia for *Crocodile Dundee* (1986)

STAGECRAFT

Why go to the trouble of transporting your actors to far-flung destination when the perfect location can be brought to them? *Star Wars* TV shows such as *The Mandalorian* (2019–) have made extensive use of Industrial Light and Magic's pioneering StageCraft technology to do exactly that. These virtual sets use giant LED screens to display digital backdrops that can be updated in real time. The visuals often feature footage captured by camera crews in actual locations, meaning the cast can "travel" thousands of miles in a matter of seconds, without leaving the studio.

eager to visit the places where their favorite moments were immortalized on-screen, the travel equivalent of buying a T-shirt or an action figure.

"There's a huge market for screen tourism and it's growing," explains Hayley Armstrong, head of production services for Creative England, an organization that helps movies and TV shows find and collaborate with their ideal locations. "Having a location used in a film or TV production can result in advertising that money just can't buy."

For much of its lifetime, cinema has given audiences a glimpse of glamorous new worlds far beyond their everyday experience. So when director William Wyler insisted on taking Audrey Hepburn and Gregory Peck to Italy for 1953's *Roman Holiday*, his radical move outside the walls of the studio created a living, breathing tourist brochure for the Italian capital.

As international travel became more accessible in the second half of the 20th century, a *Crocodile Dundee* pilgrimage to rugged Australia or a *Ghostbusters*-inspired tour of New York became a realistic option for many keen cinephiles. Meanwhile, the home entertainment revolution of the 1980s and '90s allowed fans to revisit their favorite movies whenever they wanted, ensuring the locations became even more recognizable and familiar. Even places that would never traditionally be

1992

Jurassic Park sets are wrecked when Hurricane Iniki sweeps across the Hawaiian island of Kaua'i.

2001

Peter Jackson shows that New Zealand is the perfect substitute for Middle Earth in his Oscar-winning *The Lord of the Rings* trilogy.

considered tourist destinations could become sites of pilgrimage, such as the now-demolished Acton Lane Power Station in London that was featured in both *Alien* (1979) and *Batman* (1989).

Screen tourism can be great news for a region's economy. New Zealand reportedly witnessed visitor numbers increase by 40 percent in the wake of

CINEMA HAS GIVEN AUDIENCES A GLIMPSE OF GLAMOROUS NEW WORLDS

Peter Jackson's *The Lord of the Rings* trilogy, while Highclere Castle in Hampshire, England, got a significant tourist boost from its starring role as the family home in TV hit *Downton Abbey* (2010–2015). According to tourism agency VisitEngland's figures, screen tourism brought £894 million of visitor spending to the UK in 2019. The US industry, meanwhile, is expected to double its value to $128 billion in the next decade. With streaming services

releasing an array of new content set in glorious locations around the world, trips to screen locations are only going to increase over the next few years.

While some screen tourists are happy to take a quick selfie at King's Cross station's Platform 9¾, others look for a more immersive experience. "It's down to the locations to think about how they're going to promote themselves," says Armstrong. "To have that deeper visitor experience, people want to know more about the little stories that happened on that day of filming. Anything locations can do to make a visit more immersive and interactive is

Lake Wakatipu in New Zealand, Lothlórien in *The Lord of the Rings*

2015

Suffragette becomes the first movie to shoot inside the UK's historic Houses of Parliament.

2018

Succession brings some reality to its cut-throat world by shooting boardroom scenes at 7 World Trade Center, built in 2006.

THERE IS NO SIMULATED RIVAL FOR OUR LIVING, BREATHING PLANET

really valuable." Fans of Netflix's period drama *Bridgerton* (2020–), for example, can take a full guided tour around the Bath architecture that forms the show's beautiful Georgian backdrop.

There can be a downside to screen tourism, of course. So many people wanted to follow in Leonardo DiCaprio's footsteps in *The Beach* that Thailand's spectacular Maya Bay was closed to tourists from 2018 to early 2022 to allow the coastal area to recover from severe environmental damage. Being a responsible screen traveler is now more important than ever.

As moviemaking processes and techniques continue to improve, there will be an increasing temptation to conjure entire worlds from the confines of the studio. But as countless beloved movies and TV shows have shown over

On the set of the Netflix period drama *Bridgerton* *(above)*, filmed in Bath, UK *(left)*

the years, there is no simulated rival for our living, breathing planet. Sometimes the greatest cinematic journeys can be undertaken without the need of a green screen.

2021

Following the success of *The White Lotus,* the Four Seasons San Domenico Palace in Sicily is booked up for months.

2022

Netflix show *Wednesday,* shot in Bucharest, boosts Romania's tourism industry.

⌾

STUDIO TOURS

Visiting a famous location may feel like the most obvious way to see where our favorite movies were made, but there is another way to relive those memorable moments. Part museum, part theme park and part nostalgia trip, some studios open their doors to give fans a glimpse behind the scenes.

HOLLYWOOD STUDIO TOURS, US

LA has always been the spiritual home of the American movie industry, so it's not surprising that it's packed with studio tours. Warner Bros., Sony Pictures, Paramount, and Universal all offer trips around their back lots. With each hosting a collection of iconic sets and classic props, why not get closer to some of your favorites?

HOBBITON™ MOVIE SET, NEW ZEALAND

The Lord of the Rings was such a big deal for New Zealand that an actual government minister was given responsibility for capitalizing on the movies' success. Two decades later, you can still experience the trilogy's legacy, most notably on a tour of the Hobbiton™ sets (in Matamata, Waikato) used to create the Shire™.

CINECITTÀ, ITALY

Arguably the place to go if you're looking for cinematic history, Rome's Cinecittà was built by Mussolini in the 1930s and it remains the biggest movie studio in Europe. It's played host to Federico Fellini epics and Martin Scorsese's *Gangs of New York* (2002), and the tour features a trip around the ancient Rome set built for HBO/BBC drama *Rome* (2005–2007).

GAME OF THRONES STUDIO TOUR, UK

A great deal of filming for *Game of Thrones* (2011–2019) took place in Northern Ireland, both on location and in the studio. This Banbridge-based tour puts Westerosi props, costumes, and vast sets under one roof, alongside some fun interactive exhibits. And yes, you do get to see the coveted Iron Throne in all its austere glory.

WARNER BROS. STUDIO TOUR LONDON, UK

Subtitled "The Making of Harry Potter," this studio tour in Leavesden is a must for anyone who's ever dreamed of attending Hogwarts School of Witchcraft and Wizardry. From wandering through the ramshackle streets of Diagon Alley to flying your own broomstick, this is movie magic in the most literal sense.

1

WITH GREAT POWER

Our favorite tales of good vanquishing evil often play out on streets much like those we know and love. It's this clash of the extraordinary with the ordinary that heightens the stakes and makes every larger-than-life battle seem completely believable. Yes, Spider-Man can sling his webs and Superman can take to the skies, but Peter Parker must navigate curfews and Clark Kent has deadlines to meet.

When it comes to taking comic book capers to the big screen, the choice of setting is, of course, vital. Sure, CGI use is inevitable in a genre where superheroes can fly, but the bulk of the believability behind DC's dark streets and Marvel's multicolored universe comes from the reach-out-and-touch-it realness of the locations in which they're set.

MARVEL CINEMATIC UNIVERSE

Dominating 21st-century cinema, the Marvel universe has few
rivals. This mega franchise continues to produce blockbuster hits,
bringing some of Hollywood's greatest actors along for the ride.

Dazzling New York City, home to a plethora of heroes

YEAR
2008-

LOCATION
WORLDWIDE

To say that Marvel has had a big impact on cinematic history is an understatement. The studio is a colossus, pumping out well over 50 hugely successful movies and TV shows, casting a host of renowned Hollywood stars, and changing the face of the popcorn blockbuster irrevocably.

Few would have imagined its impact when, in 2008, independent production company Marvel Studios released its very first cinematic entry, *Iron Man*. The movie was a gamble, with the main character played by then-controversial Robert Downey Jr. and the director, Jon Favreau, an unexpected choice. Against the odds, *Iron Man* took the world by storm and kick-started the studio's cinematic reign. That's not to say that superhero movies were a novelty. Before the first *Iron Man* spawned a franchise, audiences had enjoyed the likes of Christopher Reeve's heroic *Superman (p34)*, Sam Raimi's *Spider-Man* trilogy, and the *X-Men (p30)* movie series. But Marvel's box office hits were to become a force to be reckoned with.

While Marvel has become known for its extensive use of the green screen to build its sprawling universe, the success of the franchise can also be attributed to its Earth-bound location shots (after all, there couldn't be a neighborhood Spider-Man if there wasn't a—real—neighborhood). And if there was ever a city to claim Marvel's heart, it would be New York. The comic book publisher started life here in 1939 (originally as Timely Publications) and its legendary writer-editor Stan Lee, who created many of the world's favorite superheroes in the 1960s, was born in Manhattan. Lee regularly set stories in the city and based many of his heroes here (Spider-Man was

Grand Central Terminal, where the Battle of New York takes place

born and bred in Queens, Captain America hailed from Brooklyn, and Jessica Jones worked in Hell's Kitchen). By grounding his heroes in these real-life locations, and having them fight to save real places, Lee upped the stakes of his stories. On-screen, there's no better example than when the Avengers come together to fight the Chitauri, an evil alien race spearheaded by the trickster god Loki, during the climactic Battle of New York in smash-hit *The Avengers* (2012).

While the destructive Leviathan (huge armored beasts used by the Chitauri) wreak havoc over the city, the action is largely set on New York's Park Avenue Viaduct above 42nd Street, just outside the historic Grand Central Terminal (though filming mainly took place in Cleveland). Fun fact: when fans see Grand Central in the Avengers' second outing, *Age of Ultron* (2015), the clock

on the station's facade has been rebuilt with a tribute to the human forces of the Battle of New York, replacing the Greek gods on the beautiful Tiffany Clock. It's a superb little detail added by the Marvel graphics gurus.

While Grand Central Terminal is a landmark of New York, the building isn't Loki's true target. In fact, the God of Mischief has his sights set firmly on Stark Tower. Tony Stark's shimmering skyscraper, which became the Avengers Tower by the time of *Captain America: The Winter Soldier* (2014), is actually a CGI top superimposed on the MetLife Building. James Chinlund, production designer on *The Avengers,* grew up in New York and saw this 59-story building every day. He told *Gizmodo* in 2012 that it was the perfect place to fuse old New York with the futuristic tech of the MCU. "Tony Stark bought the iconic MetLife Building and ripped

in the Appel Room at the Deutsche Bank Center in *The Defenders* (2017).

② Central Park

③ New York Philharmonic

HELL'S KITCHEN

④ Rockefeller Center

Queensboro Bridge ⑤

⑨ Times Square

MIDTOWN EAST

MIDTOWN WEST

MetLife Building ⑥

⑧ Park Ave. Viaduct ⑦ Grand Central Terminal

MANHATTAN

QUEENS

Hudson River

East River

CHELSEA

Flatiron Building ⑩

GRAMERCY PARK

GREENWICH VILLAGE

177A Bleecker St. ⑪

NEW YORK CITY

SOHO

LOWER EAST SIDE

TRIBECA

LOWER MANHATTAN

WILLIAMSBURG

DUMBO

BROOKLYN

⑫ Staten Island Ferry

④ Rockefeller Center

Clint Barton, aka Hawkeye, and the ever-eager Kate Bishop end the first series of *Hawkeye* (2021–) battling the Tracksuit Mafia in the Rockefeller Plaza building, on the famous ice rink, and in the Christmas tree. The seasonal New York area was recreated in an Atlanta sound stage using digital scans of the real-life location.

⑤

Queensboro Bridge

Spider-Man and MJ are surrounded by press helicopters on top of the Queensboro Bridge at the start of *Spider-Man: No Way Home*.

⑥ MetLife Building

Tony Stark's high-tech HQ (Stark Tower, later known as Avengers Tower) is digitally imposed on the MetLife Building. Parts of the real lower floors can be seen merged into the structure.

⑦ Grand Central Terminal

During the epic Battle of New York in *The Avengers*, this station is damaged by a hulking Leviathan.

⑧ Park Ave. Viaduct

After crashing a Quinjet in front of 101 Park Ave. (which is featured in other movies, such as *Gremlins 2*) the Avengers assemble on this roadway.

①

Alexander Hamilton Bridge

Peter Parker first meets the universe-hopping Doctor Octopus in *Spider-Man: No Way Home* (2021) on this bridge (filmed in Atlanta).

② Central Park

At the end of *The Avengers,* the team watch Thor return to Asgard with a captured Loki from Bethesda Terrace in Central Park.

③ New York Philharmonic

Alexandra has a private performance from the New York Philharmonic

⑨

Times Square

A confused Steve Rogers (aka Captain America) runs into the center of Times Square after waking from his 70 years in ice in *Captain America: The First Avenger* (2011).

⑩ Flatiron Building

This 22-story landmark is home to Damage Control, the officious baddies from *Ms. Marvel* (2022). In the Sam Raimi *Spider-Man* movies, it's *Daily Bugle* HQ.

⑪ 177A Bleecker St.

Perhaps the most famous street address in the Marvel universe, 177A Bleecker St. is the home to sorcerer Doctor Strange.

⑫

Staten Island Ferry

Midway through *Spider-Man: Homecoming* (2017), Peter tries to catch the villainous Vulture on the Staten Island Ferry, flouting Iron Man's instruction to keep a low profile.

off the top, adding his own piece of parasitic architecture to the top" the production designer speculated. Eagle-eyed fans will notice that the entire MetLife Building is once again visible in the final episode of *Hawkeye* and in the second *Doctor Strange* movie. In this universe, perhaps MetLife gets the building back after the Avengers have relocated upstate? Just south of this building is 101 Park Avenue, where the Quinjet aircraft carrying a ready-to-fight Black Widow, Hawkeye, and Captain America smashes down in *The Avengers*.

The Avengers may have assembled, but where was the powerful Doctor Strange while the gang were battling the Chitauri? As we later learn, Earth's primary protector wasn't, in fact, a sorcerer at this point in time, and it's the Ancient One that fans watch fighting off the aliens at the sorcerer's 177A Bleecker Street home in the finale, *Avengers: Endgame* (2019). This has been the official address of Doctor Strange since a telegram addressed to the Sanctum Sanctorum was spotted in September 1969's *Doctor Strange #182* comic. It was always an inside joke between Marvel writers Roy Thomas and Gary Friedrich and artist Bill Everett, who had lived at 177 Bleecker Street; Stan Lee's regular collaborator Steve Ditko also lived near here and knew the street well. These days, the 19th-century tenement block has a bodega on the ground floor; you can grab a snack here for an authentic New York City experience, but you're unlikely to spot Doctor Strange in the neighborhood.

In reality, the impressive interior of the Sanctum Sanctorum was shot in the UK, on a set at Longcross Studios, just outside London. The glass-roofed courtyard of the huge British Museum, meanwhile, served as Earth-838's New York Illuminati HQ in *Doctor Strange in the Multiverse of Madness* (2022).

This wasn't the first time England doubled for New York in the Marvel universe. For Captain America's origin story, *Captain America: The First Avenger* (2011), Marvel Studios used the historic streets of Manchester and Liverpool to recreate World War II–era Brooklyn. When Steve Rogers emerges from the super-soldier experiment (taller and stronger than ever before), he springs straight into action, chasing an assassin through the streets of Brooklyn and along the docks – in reality, the mid-19th-century Stanley Dock in Liverpool.

Cleveland, Ohio, also subbed in for the Big Apple during the Avengers' Battle of New York. The team-up sequence was filmed on East 9th Street, in Cleveland's downtown area, with the studio digitally inserting the New York background during postproduction, including the facade of Grand Central Terminal. The city also stands in for New York during the *Captain America* sequel (2014) and in the earlier non-MCU *Spider-Man 3* (2007). Why does Cleveland make such a good substitute for the Big Apple? The American city is in the same East Coast time zone, architecturally similar and has far less traffic, meaning it's easier to shut down roads for filming.

The courtyard of the British Museum, aka Illuminati HQ

SPIDEY IN SCHOOL

To prepare for his role as Spider-Man, Tom Holland secretly went undercover in a Bronx high school to experience life in the American education system. He got bored on his second day and started telling everyone why he was really there.

New York's MetLife Building, upon which Stark Tower sits in the Marvel universe

① San Francisco
The spectacular bus fight in *Shang-Chi and the Legend of the Ten Rings* (2021) passes though Ghirardelli Square and the Stockton Street Tunnel before ending at North Point and Larkin streets.

②

Shaver Lake
This picturesque lake in California was the isolated crash site of Carol Danvers and Mar-Vell in *Captain Marvel* (2019).

③ Edwards Air Force Base
This high-security base was the location for airfield scenes in *Captain Marvel*.

④ Los Angeles
When Nick Fury asks Stark to "exit the donut" in *Iron Man 2* (2010), Stark is resting on top of Randy's Donuts in Inglewood.

In *Iron Man 3*, Happy Hogan narrowly escapes an explosion at the ornate Grauman's Chinese Theatre on Hollywood Boulevard.

The Blockbuster Video store that Vers crashes into in *Captain Marvel* was built at a closed store at 6321 Laurel Canyon Boulevard, North Hollywood.

⑤ NY-97
Stephen Strange loses control of his car on New York State Route 97 near the "Hawk's Nest" section of road during the start of the first *Doctor Strange* movie.

⑥

Cleveland
As well as doubling for New York, Cleveland also became Stuttgart in *The Avengers*. It's here that Loki forces a crowd to kneel before him in Cleveland's Public Square.

⑦ Washington, DC
Captain America meets Sam Wilson on an early morning run around Washington, DC's Reflecting Pool and Jefferson Memorial in the opening scene of *The Winter Soldier*.

⑧ Rose Hill
Iron Man gets stranded in a town called Rose Hill in *Iron Man 3*. The town is based on a real place, but it's really in North Carolina rather than Tennessee, as it appears in the movie.

⑨

Atlanta
The city's striking High Museum of Art becomes the fictional Museum of Great Britain in *Black Panther*.

Atlanta Marriott Marquis's unique interior was used as the TVA Headquarters in *Loki* (2021–).

In *Captain America: Civil War* (2016) and *Spider-Man: Homecoming*, Avengers HQ was the digitally enhanced Porsche Experience Center in Atlanta.

Wheat Street Tower plays a housing block in Oakland, California, at the start and end of *Black Panther*.

⑩ Bouckaert Farm
This farm in Georgia was the grassy setting for the battle scenes in *Avengers: Infinity War* (2018) and *Black Panther*. The estate also hosts Tony Stark's cabin in *Avengers: Endgame*; luckily for fans, it's available to rent.

⑪

Vizcaya Museum and Gardens
Iron Man 3's Mandarin broadcasts from this early 20th-century estate in Miami, Florida.

While New York City is the center of the Marvel universe, it's not the only place our heroes call home—after all, if you can fly, why stick to one place? Tony Stark's Malibu mansion isn't a real address, but there are plenty of other MCU locations around California. In Hollywood, fans can visit the historic Grauman's Chinese Theatre, where an Extremis explosion in *Iron Man 3* (2013) nearly kills Happy—filming here closed Hollywood Boulevard for two days. In 2010's *Iron Man 2*, Nick Fury finds the hero sitting inside the giant doughnut on the roof of Randy's Donuts near Los Angeles International Airport (LAX).

Washington, DC, has also appeared throughout the franchise. You can race around the US capital's picturesque Reflecting Pool, just like Steve "on your left" Rogers and Sam Wilson do when they first meet in *The Winter Soldier*.

The Reflecting Pool, a pleasant spot for a run

Alternatively, follow Peter Parker on his school trip to the nearby Washington Monument, which features in a tense scene during *Spider-Man: Homecoming* (2017), although the action was shot with a green screen.

Lucky Peter jets off on another school trip in his second outing, *Spider-Man: Far From Home* (2019), this time to Europe. Fans can visit the beautiful

A BASE FOR THE MCU

Camp Lehigh, a fictional military base in New Jersey, has popped up multiple times in the MCU but has been filmed at a number of locations. Black Park forest, next to Pinewood Studios in London, serves as the 1940s setting for Steve Rogers's training in *Captain America: The First Avenger*, while the 1970s version of the camp in *Avengers: Endgame* was shot at an old warehouse complex on Sylvan Road Southwest, in Atlanta.

Grauman's Chinese Theatre, the site of an explosion in *Iron Man 3*

Charles Bridge, where MJ discovers Peter's real identity, or stay in the luxury NH Collection Prague Carlo IV hotel the kids end up in, both in the Czech capital. The scorching Elemental fight, however, was filmed in the city of Liberec, some 80 miles (128 km) away. After his trip to Prague, Peter travels to Berlin before joining his classmates in London. It's in the UK capital that *Far From Home* concludes, with the famous Tower Bridge *(p32)* taking center stage in the final fight against the charming, but villainous Mysterio. What audiences see on-screen is, in fact, a digital model of the landmark bridge. A number of key places in *Eternals* (2021), which director Chloé Zhao largely shot on location, can also be found around the UK capital. Popular areas such as Camden High Street, Piccadilly Circus, and Hampstead Heath appear as the emphathetic Sersi tries to get the godly group back together.

As Marvel's universe has expanded, and the reach of its super-powered characters with it, the studio's location scouts have had to go global. Stunning locations in the US were used to create Black Panther's Wakanda, with a farm in Georgia standing in for its grassy plains in *Infinity War*, but it was Argentina's Iguazú Falls that inspired Warrior Falls, where the battle for the crown takes place in *Black Panther* (2018). Thanos's "Garden" in the Avengers' final two movies was set in the gorgeous Banaue Rice Terraces in the Philippines.

While green screens have become a foundation for the Marvel universe—particularly when the heroes space-hop around various planets—the inspiration behind these fantastical places largely comes from Earth. With its huge wealth of historic landmarks and spectacular natural landscapes, it's little wonder the Avengers assemble to protect our humble planet.

Thanos's "Garden," the Banaue Rice Terraces in the Philippines

① **Hjørundfjorden**
Black Widow hides in Norway in her self-titled movie (2021) and is shown crossing snowy Hjørundfjorden on a ferry.

② **Liberec**
Spider-Man and Mysterio fight the fire Elemental in Dr. Edvard Beneše Square in Liberec (pretending to be Prague), in *Spider-Man: Far From Home*.

③ **Prague**
MJ discovers some suspicious-looking tech upon Prague's landmark Charles Bridge in *Far From Home*.

While on their school trip, Peter and his classmates end up staying at the NH Collection Prague Carlo IV hotel.

Peter's fellow students are forced to watch an opera at the ornate Vinohrady Theatre instead of joining the city's lively carnival celebrations.

④ **Campo Santa Maria Formosa**
The battle with the water Elemental in *Spider-Man: Far From Home* was shot in this square; it's here that Spider-Man tries to save the bell tower.

⑤

Forte di Bard
This imposing fortress in Italy stood in for HYDRA's Sokovian HQ in *Avengers: Age of Ultron*.

⑥ **Belchite**
In *Spider-Man: No Way Home*, viewers first see an Elemental in the village of Ixtenco, Mexico. The filming actually took place in Belchite (p68) in Spain.

⑦ **Salisbury Plain**
Ajak's sweeping South Dakota ranch in *Eternals* was filmed on Salisbury Plain, near the prehistoric Stonehenge monument.

⑧

Sainsbury Centre
Appearing in *Avengers: Age of Ultron*, this modernist art gallery in Norwich was the first incarnation of the Avengers compound.

⑨ **St. Abbs**
This tiny fishing village in Scotland became New Asgard in *Avengers: Endgame*; it's here fans meet a much-changed Thor.

⑩

Edinburgh
Wanda and Vision stroll (and fight for their lives) through this stunning Scottish city at the beginning of *Avengers: Infinity War*.

⑪ **Camden High St.**
The *Eternals* battle a monstrous Deviant that makes its way onto Camden High Street; it's here that Sersi turns a bright red bus into a flurry of rose petals.

⑫ **British Museum**
In his second movie, Doctor Strange is brought before the Illuminati in the British Museum.

⑬ **Piccadilly Circus**
In *Eternals*, fans meet Sersi in central London's Piccadilly Circus. She then walks into the main hall of the city's grand Natural History Museum, actually in South Kensington.

⑭ **Tower Bridge**
Far From Home ends in a battle above the British capital's Tower Bridge (which was digitally recreated for the movie).

⑮

Old Royal Naval College
Evil Malekith lands his gigantic spaceship at Greenwich Naval College in *Thor: The Dark World* (2013).

LONDON
⑪ Camden High St.
⑫ British Museum
⑬ Piccadilly Circus
⑭ Tower Bridge
Thames
River
Old Royal Naval College ⑮

Hjørundfjorden ①
FINLAND
NORWAY   SWEDEN
ESTONIA
Edinburgh ⑩ ⑨ St. Abbs
DENMARK   LITHUANIA
UNITED KINGDOM
BELARUS
IRELAND   Sainsbury ⑧ Centre
GERMANY   POLAND
Salisbury Plain ⑦   See London inset map, above
② Liberec
FRANCE   Prague ③ CZECH REPUBLIC   UKRAINE
AUSTRIA
ROMANIA
Forte di Bard ⑤   ④ Campo Santa Maria Formosa
ITALY   BULGARIA
Belchite ⑥
PORTUGAL   TURKEY
SPAIN   GREECE

X-MEN

Superhero adaptations were far from surefire hits at the turn of the millennium, but the *X-Men* movies showed how real-life locations can help make the unbelievable believable.

YEAR
2000–

LOCATION
CANADA; ENGLAND; AUSTRALIA

If superheroes have now become the defining genre of 21st-century Hollywood, the first *X-Men* (2000) was instrumental in beginning the revolution. Arriving three years after the critically derided *Batman & Robin*, the hit Marvel feature took its source material suitably seriously. In fact, its nuanced story owed plenty to the American Civil Rights movement that had inspired original creators Stan Lee and Jack Kirby back in the 1960s.

The filmmakers took care to ensure their first mutant trilogy was set in a plausible near-future by using plenty of real-life locations in Canada. The Parkwood Estate in Oshawa was the exterior for Professor Xavier's School for Gifted Youngsters in the first movie, and the vast Kananaskis Lakes in Alberta became the perfect setting for Alkali Lake (the place of Wolverine's "birth") in *X2* (2003). When the movie saga required climactic scenes to be based in iconic real-life sites, such as the Statue of Liberty or Alcatraz Island, locations in Ontario and British Columbia, respectively, filled in.

As the franchise grew to include a number of prequels, a Wolverine trilogy and the comedic spin-off *Deadpool* (2016), production bases in Australia and the UK were added to the roster. Although Hugh Jackman did make it to

Tokyo for 2013's *The Wolverine* (a loose take on a beloved Japan-set comic-book arc), many of the movie's key scenes were actually shot in Sydney.

Locations throughout the *X-Men* movies are far from consistent, however. The saga has a convoluted, occasionally contradictory continuity, and this can often be reflected in changes to certain key backdrops. For example, when fans see Professor Xavier's school in the 1960s-set prequel *First Class* (2011), it's really a building in England (Englefield House near Reading), not Canada.

Nonetheless, the saga's noticeably realistic approach proved that Marvel's set of superheroes could be extremely bankable on the big screen, paving the way for the all-conquering Marvel Cinematic Universe *(p20)*.

Parkwood Estate, the location of Professor Xavier's School for Gifted Youngsters

DID YOU KNOW?

DOUGRAY SCOTT
Scottish actor Dougray Scott was lined up to play Wolverine until his commitments on *Mission: Impossible II (p210)* got in the way.

HUGH JACKMAN
Jackman is significantly taller than the comic-book Wolverine—who is 5 ft 3in (1.6 m)—so the filmmakers tried to make him look as short as possible in the first movie.

A BRIDGE TOO FAR

Bridges are just a way of crossing water, right? Not on screen. Often destroyed, sometimes saved, but rarely walked across, these bridges have been featured in unforgettable movie moments.

GOLDEN GATE BRIDGE, US

Despite its sturdy construction, this is supposedly the most destroyed bridge on screen. It was ripped up and moved in *X-Men: The Last Stand* (2006), was a ruinous battleground in *Rise of the Planet of the Apes* (2011), and has been shattered by innumerable earthquakes and monsters—who can forget the *kaiju* assault in *Pacific Rim* (2013)?

TOWER BRIDGE, UK

London's most famous bridge has graced the screen in countless scene-stealing performances. Key climactic battle scenes were set here for both *Sherlock Holmes* (2009) and *Spider-Man: Far From Home (p28)*. The latter brilliantly combined footage filmed on studio sets with an intricate CGI model created by digitally scanning every element of the bridge over 10 days.

BROOKLYN BRIDGE, US

With the Manhattan skyline as a backdrop, this New York landmark was made for the screen. Yet its scenic splendor hasn't prevented it from being attacked by monsters and missiles alike, including in *Godzilla* (1998) and

I Am Legend (2007). Thankfully, it hasn't all been carnage; the animated heroes of *Oliver and Company* (1988) used the bridge's cables to escape the pursuit of the nefarious Bill Sykes.

PONT DE BIR-HAKEIM, FRANCE

Directors must have decided that this two-tiered marvel—with its classical style and soaring colonnades—was too beautiful to be destroyed. Instead, it has provided the setting for a morose Marlon Brando stroll in *Last Tango in Paris* (1972) and a mind-altering sequence in *Inception* (2010). So captivating was the bridge in the latter that it became known as "The Inception Bridge."

EDMUND PETTUS BRIDGE, US

It may have been featured in only a few movies, but Edmund Pettus Bridge carries a whole lot of historical weight. Nearly 50 years after the events of "Bloody Sunday," director Ava Duverney spent four days shooting at this spot, expertly recreating the Civil Rights marches across the bridge as part of her Oscar-winning film *Selma* (2014).

1 Golden Gate Bridge standing tall and strong, unlike in so many movies

2 London's Tower Bridge, without a superhero or super-sleuth in sight

3 An emblem of New York City, the Brooklyn Bridge

4 The grand colonnades of Pont de Bir-Hakeim

5 Alabama's Edmund Pettus Bridge today, a National Historic Landmark

1

2

3

4 **5**

SUPERMAN

Fighting for truth, justice, and the American way, the original spandex-wearing superhero was brought to the big screen in 1978, setting the standard for superhero movies that followed.

YEAR
1978, 1980,
1983, 1987

LOCATION
US

Was there a better person to play Superman? Bringing an earnest charm to the role, Christopher Reeve's portrayal of the man of steel is still a highlight of the superhero genre, and the movies in which he starred remain favorites among fans.

Though much of the Reeves-era Superman movies were filmed in Pinewood Studios, in England, location shoots in the US were used to bring the fictional Smallville and Metropolis to life. The city of Metropolis, where our hero Clark Kent and reporter Lois Lane live and work, was first named in Action Comics #16, and while its exact location is left ambiguous, it's often compared to New York's Manhattan. It made sense, then, for director Richard Donner to capture key scenes on the bustling streets of the Big Apple. The city's *Daily News* skyscraper became the offices of the *Daily Planet*, its Art Deco building, standing 36 stories high, an ideal backdrop for that famous helicopter scene. Here's a tidbit: while filming here in July 1977, the infamous New York blackout struck, plunging the city into darkness. The production crew lent their lights to the *Daily News* team to help get the paper to press. Now there's an act of kindness Superman would be proud of.

①
San Francisco
In the first movie, Superman saves a school bus on the edge of the Golden Gate Bridge; the action was filmed on a model in the UK.

③

Glen Canyon
This natural landscape is where villainous CEO Webster and programmer Gus Gorman build their supercomputer in *Superman III*.

②

Hoover Dam
As a result of Lex Luthor's plans in the first movie, the Hoover Dam collapses. Although a model was used in the movie, the team also included footage of the dam.

⑤
New York City
The *Daily News* office on 42nd St. became *Daily Planet* HQ.

Lex Luthor's secret lair was set in an abandoned tunnel beneath Grand Central Terminal.

④
Superman Canyon Rd.
This aptly renamed road in New Mexico is where Lois and her car succumb to the earthquake in *Superman*.

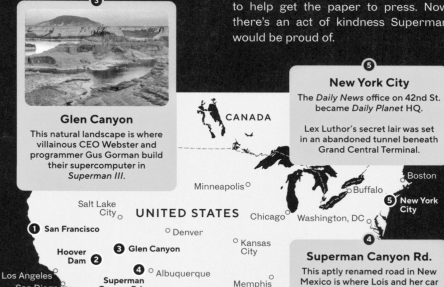

CANADA

Boston

Minneapolis

Buffalo

Salt Lake City

UNITED STATES

Chicago

Washington, DC

⑤ New York City

Denver

① San Francisco

Kansas City

Hoover Dam **②**

③ Glen Canyon

④ Albuquerque

Los Angeles

San Diego

Superman Canyon Rd.

Memphis

Dallas

MEXICO

Houston

BATMAN

Director Tim Burton's predilection for the moody and Gothic found its perfect match in DC's Gotham, creating a new vision for Batman that felt worlds away from the family-friendly 1960s series.

YEAR
1989

LOCATION
ENGLAND

While flashy Manhattan may have inspired Superman's city Metropolis, Batman's infamous Gotham City draws on New York's bleaker underbelly, a match for the movie's gloomy anti-hero. Bringing Gotham to the big screen, therefore, demanded a director with an edge.

Admittedly, there was concern that Tim Burton, a young director of two offbeat comedies, should be handed such a huge project. But inspired by contemporary portrayals of the caped crusader, such as Frank Miller's comic book series *The Dark Knight Returns* (1986) and Alan Moore's *Batman: The*

Killing Joke (1988), Burton developed the gritty and Gothic city everyone wanted.

Though he filmed most scenes on sound stages at England's Pinewood Studios, Burton turned to industrial sites and Gothic manors to establish the movie's dark tone. For Bruce Wayne/Batman's Wayne Manor, two country houses in Hertfordshire, Knebworth and Hatfield, stood in for the exterior and interior. The first big set piece, the ambush of the soon-to-be Joker at Axis Chemical Works, took place at Little Barford Power Station in Cambridge and the Acton Lane Power Station (now demolished) in London. Much like Batman, Burton was well suited to the shadows, and his successful vision set a darker tone for the superhero movies of the future.

Knebworth House, a suitably Gothic stand-in for the exterior of Wayne Manor

Chicago's La Salle Street, prominently featured in the trilogy

1

Lower Wacker Dr.

Batman chases the Joker along this road in *The Dark Knight* (2008); the adjacent Franklin-Orleans St. Bridge leads to "The Narrows" area of Gotham.

2

Richard J. Daley Center

Wayne Enterprises is based in this soaring skyscraper. In reality, the building is the City of Chicago's main civic center.

3

Navy Pier

Gotham's terrified residents are evacuated onto ferries at this pier during the Joker's attack in *The Dark Knight*.

4

La Salle St.

A police memorial is attacked on this street in *The Dark Knight*, which is also where the Batman and the Joker first meet.

5

Old Post Office

The memorable bank heist at the beginning of *The Dark Knight* was filmed in the Old Post Office on Van Buren St. The exterior is the northern corner at W Van Buren St. and Canal St.

KINZIE   STREET

FULTON
MARKET

RANDOLPH   STREET

KENNEDY   EXPRESSWAY

ADAMS   STREET

EISENHOWER   EXPRESSWAY

HALSTED   STREET

*University
of Illinois*

GRAND   AVENUE

RIVER
NORTH

MICHIGAN   AVE

STREETERVILLE

Navy Pier **3**

Chicago   River

Richard J. Daley
Center

Lower
Wacker Dr. **1**

RANDOLPH   STREET

2   STREET

LOOP

La Salle St. **5**

ADAMS   STREET

Old Post
Office **5**

CHICAGO

CANAL   STREET

HARRISON   STREET

SOUTH
LOOP

MICHIGAN   AVENUE

GRANT
PARK

LAKE SHORE DRIVE

THE DARK KNIGHT TRILOGY

Grounding Batman and his foes in a familiar-looking city with equally familiar themes, Christopher Nolan's *Dark Knight* trilogy didn't just entertain audiences, it asked questions of them, too.

YEAR
2005, 2008, 2012

LOCATION
WORLDWIDE

Before there was Batman, there was Bruce Wayne. How did an orphaned millionaire, full of fear, become the "hero Gotham deserves"? For director Christopher Nolan, then a relative newcomer, the chance to explore the Batman myth was a far more interesting prospect than creating another comic book caper—and fortunately Warner Bros. agreed.

Something of an outlier in the superhero movie landscape, *The Dark Knight* trilogy has more in common with action thrillers than it does with the on-screen antics of Spider-Man, Superman, and co. There's a realism to Nolan's approach, something achieved in large part by on-location shoots. The director selected Chicago (and later Pittsburgh) to stand-in for Gotham, supplementing the city with parts of London. Chicago's clean architectural lines and lack of notable landmarks provided a blank canvas: its streets were primed for Batman's "Tumbler" (the hero's mode of transportation) to speed through and its hulking buildings (such as the Old Chicago Main Post Office) were ideal for slick bank robberies and Wayne Enterprises meetings. Over in the UK, full use was made of the country's architecture. St.

Pancras Renaissance Hotel in London and Abbey Mills Pumping Station (a beautiful Victorian sewage facility) were repurposed—and made suitably grittier—to play Arkham Asylum, while various stately homes stood in for the interior and exterior of Wayne Manor.

Ever the perfectionist, Nolan had no second unit and directed every moment of production, which, over three movies, took him not just to Chicago, Pittsburgh and the UK, but all over the world. *Batman Begins* had sequences on the Vatnajökull glacier in Iceland, *The Dark Knight* travels to the vast International Finance Center in Hong Kong, and *The Dark Knight Rises* features scenes at the

East London's Abbey Mills Pumping Station, which doubled as Arkham Asylum

37

SAFETY FIRST

Mehrangarh Fort in Jodhpur, northwest India. These places, with their unique architecture and natural light, meant special effects could be used sparingly (in stark contrast to the superhero movies of the future); Nolan seamlessly added Nepalese temples to footage he shot in Iceland, for example, and crafted miniatures to get the shots he needed when filming in real life wasn't an option.

And it's this fastidious attention to detail that placed Gotham in the here and now. Nolan created a city that audiences could easily imagine visiting, perhaps working in, and in so doing made every character's story arc believable and the moral dilemmas posed talking points. When the Joker rigs two boats with explosives and gives the passengers on each the detonator, we're there with them on the boat, debating what we should do. When Bane and his anarchic crew overthrow the rich and powerful, we can't help but wonder where things go from here. Thanks to Nolan's dedication to keeping things real, Batman's fight to save Gotham is truly worth investing in right up to the final frame.

Wollaton Hall in Nottinghamshire, repurposed for Wayne Manor in *The Dark Knight Rises*

Derby ○ ❶ Wollaton Hall

○ Leicester

○ Peterborough

Norwich ○

○ Coventry

ENGLAND

○ Cambridge

Milton Keynes ○

❷ Cardington

Ipswich ○

Mentmore ❸
Towers

Oxford ○

St Albans ○

○ Chelmsford

Osterley ❹   ❺ London
House

○ Southend

Reading ○

Canterbury ○

○ Guildford   Maidstone ○

Dover ○

○ Southampton

Brighton ○   ○ Hastings

① Wollaton Hall
The exterior shots of Wayne Manor were relocated to this Tudor stately home for *The Dark Knight Rises* (2012).

Osterley House
This opulent house was used for the Wayne Manor interior scenes in *The Dark Knight Rises*.

**② **

Cardington
Nolan made frequent use of the cavernous Cardington airship hangars in Bedfordshire, notably for the plane scene and Bane's lair in *The Dark Knight Rises*.

③ Mentmore Towers
The ill-fated Wayne Manor in *Batman Begins* is Mentmore Towers in Buckinghamshire. It is currently being transformed into a hotel.

**④ **

⑤ London
The Senate House appears as the courthouse in *Batman Begins* (2005) and again as the setting for the masquerade ball in *The Dark Knight Rises*.

Bruce Wayne uses the ExCel London exhibition halls to test the "Tumbler" in *Batman Begins*.

The destroyed warehouse where Batman sits mournfully in *The Dark Knight* is, in fact, Battersea Power Station.

DC UNIVERSE

At first sticking to the gritty storylines of its comic book source material, the DC Universe has expanded, bringing new characters and themes, and an array of global settings, to the big screen.

YEAR
2013–

LOCATION
WORLDWIDE

What words would you use to describe the DC Universe? Brooding? Probably. Grim? Perhaps. Dark? Almost certainly. Maybe you'd use all three. And you'd have a point. From the rain-lashed streets of Gotham and Metropolis in *Man of Steel* (2013) and *Batman v Superman: Dawn of Justice* (2016), to the shadow-saturated darkness of Midtown in *Suicide Squad* (2016), there's a definite aesthetic at play across these movies, and it isn't just confined to lighting and location. Rage, murder, mental illness, genocide: these elements travel from source material to screen, setting the DC Universe at odds with much of Marvel's lighter cinematic output *(p20)*. Indeed, so grim was the look and feel of *Suicide Squad* that its director, David Ayer, had a therapist on-set should his actors need respite from the heavy script and shoots.

DC's shift to black arguably began in 1986 when comics legend Frank Miller

The Aragon Ballroom in Chicago, where Bruce Wayne's parents are murdered in *Batman v Superman*

Hamilton ④

Shazam discovers he is bullet-proof in the Busy Bee Food Mart on Barton St. East.

CANADA

Toronto ⑤

Suicide Squad used the streets and buildings of Toronto to become Midway City. The exterior of Union station was digitally enhanced to become Midway City Train Terminal.

Philadelphia ⑥

Shazam enjoys the famous *Rocky* view from the steps of the Philadelphia Museum of Art. Later he damages a bus while showing off his superpowers to strangers.

Minneapolis

Toronto ⑤

Boston

Hamilton ④

Buffalo

Lansing ②

Milwaukee

Detroit ③

Chicago ①

Philadelphia ⑥

Pittsburgh

UNITED STATES

St. Louis

Chicago ①

Bruce Wayne loses his parents outside Chicago's Aragon Ballroom in *Batman v Superman*.

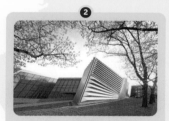

Lansing ②

Batman v Superman's Lex Luthor lives in the glass and steel Eli and Edythe Broad Art Museum in Lansing.

Detroit ③

The "Greatest Gladiator Fight in History" took place in the abandoned Michigan Central Station in Detroit during *Batman v Superman*.

In the same movie, Batman and Superman first come to blows in the Russell Industrial Center.

The Ralli Diner where Martha Wayne works in *Batman v Superman* is the Hygrade Deli on Michigan Ave.

put his now seminal Batman story *The Dark Knight Returns* down on the page. Miller transformed the biff, bam, boom, camp and color of both comic-book and 1960s TV Batman into something dark and layered. And it was Miller's take that influenced the Batman movies of Tim Burton *(p35)* and Christopher Nolan *(p36)*; you can easily draw an evolutionary line from one to the next, culminating in Zack Snyder's *Batman v Superman*. The second installment in the DC Universe, the movie owes the most obvious debt to the work of Miller, with the bulky look of Ben Affleck's Bat Suit (made from a thin carbon fiber weave to accentuate Affleck's physicality) and the superhero fight itself lifted straight from the pages of his comic book. The

movie's keenly anticipated brawl between the two protagonists was shot at the abandoned Michigan Central Station, just west of downtown Detroit. In rain-drenched darkness, of course.

And yet, for all its dark themes, as the DC Universe has expanded it has slowly let in the light, using stunning global locations and practical effects to complement its CGI, and introducing more upbeat stories and heroes. DC movies have now filmed in almost every corner of the world, from the UK, Iceland and mainland Europe to North America and Australia, creating a cornucopia of color that challenges the once muted look. While *Batman v Superman* reveled in darkness, *Shazam!*

GOTHAM AND METROPOLIS

The name Gotham has its origins in the Anglo-Saxon for "goat-town," an old, derogatory nickname for New York City. The skyline of Metropolis was originally modeled on Toronto, though the town of Metropolis, Illinois, was named the official "Home of Superman" in 1972.

① Sutton Scarsdale Hall

A digital version of this ruined stately home became the Wayne Manor in *Batman v Superman*.

② Upper Heyford

Wonder Woman's final battle at the Belgian airfield was filmed on a set at Upper Heyford airfield.

③ Hatfield House

The Long Gallery was the internal location for the German High Command gala in *Wonder Woman*. The building also played Wayne Manor in *Batman (p35)*.

④ Tilbury Docks

The walled industrial military factory being used by General Ludendorff in *Wonder Woman* was Tilbury Docks in Essex.

⑤ London

Diana's shopping trip to Selfridges was filmed in Australia House on the Strand in the first *Wonder Woman*.

Wonder Woman demonstrates her skills in the grand halls of the Old Bailey central criminal courts at the start of *Justice League*.

Diana samples her first ice cream at Paddington station—in reality, King's Cross station—in *Wonder Woman*.

⑥ Bourne Wood

Diana's team travel on horseback here to reach the German High Command in *Wonder Woman*.

⑦ Arundel Castle

In *Wonder Woman,* the exterior of the building that hosts the German gala was filmed at the spectacular Arundel Castle. *Doctor Who (p180)* also filmed here in 1988.

Map labels:

Derby
Leicester
Peterborough
Coventry
ENGLAND
Milton Keynes
Cambridge
① Sutton Scarsdale Hall
② Upper Heyford
③ Hatfield House
Tilbury Docks
London
④
⑤
Reading
Bourne Wood ⑥
Guildford
Southampton
Arundel Castle ⑦
Brighton

Bourne Wood, which appears in *Wonder Woman*

(2019) sped toward the light; where *Man of Steel* was serious, *Wonder Woman* (2017) was campy; and while *Suicide Squad* was a bit of a bumpy ride, its reincarnation *The Suicide Squad* (2021) was far smoother.

While making the reboot of *Suicide Squad*, director James Gunn cut down on the use of CGI, used as many practical effects as he could, and built sets—those sets became one of the largest construction projects in Warner Bros. history. The team also shot on location in sunny Panama. The result is a movie of vivid action with a pulsing color palette that instantly gave the franchise a new lease on life.

The Italian city of Matera, a building block of Themyscira

Nowhere is DC's approach to location filming more evident than in the tour de force *Wonder Woman*, which promises an almost perfect, narrative-boosting synergy between theme and setting. The beautiful Italian towns of Matera—also explored by James Bond in *No Time to Die (p190)*—Ravello and Palinuro, the latter two dotted along the picture-perfect Amalfi coastline, stand in for the mythical kingdom of Themyscira. The movie's early sun-soaked scenes provide a contrast with the dark and desperate landscapes of war-torn Europe into which Diana Prince later travels. Perhaps aptly—considering DC's juggling acts with the tone of its movies—one

of the biggest logistical challenges the director of photography faced while filming the Amazons vs. Germans beach battle was keeping the lighting levels consistent over two long weeks of changing weather conditions.

Wonder Woman's climax sees the warm light of dawn breaking across the inky-black sky, signifying both the end of war and the resolution of Diana's internal struggle. In that moment, she learns how to let the light in, something the movie, and the DC Extended Universe itself, has successfully sought to do. And with a fresh batch of movies slated for release, DC might be ready to steal the spotlight from Marvel.

R-RATING

The Director's Cut of *Batman v Superman* was so brutal that it became the first Batman or Superman feature to earn an R-rating from the Motion Picture Association of America.

AMNESTY BAY

Aquaman's town in Maine, which is first seen in *Justice League* (2017), was actually filmed in the tiny village of Djúpavík in Iceland.

ROLLER SKATING

Filming for *Birds of Prey*'s roller skating scene went surprisingly smoothly, partly because Margot Robbie had skating skills from her *I, Tonya* (2017) training.

BOURNE WOOD

A leafy heathland tucked away in Surrey, England, this nature spot has doubled as a favorite movie location ever since scenes for the blockbuster *Gladiator* were shot here.

Nature lovers and filmmakers alike can be found roaming around this forest, seeking out its unspoiled wooded paths and sweeping vistas. Bourne Wood is secluded, with an untouched and wild beauty that makes it a malleable backdrop for scenes of times gone by. Since 1999, it has provided the setting for many a movie, transporting viewers everywhere from medieval England to ancient Germania.

And the superhero genre has caught on, too. The wood's looming trees are featured in one of the first Marvel movies, *Captain America: The First Avenger* (2011), with *Thor: The Dark World* (2013) and *Avengers: Age of Ultron* (2015) following suit. There's no franchise loyalty, though—in 2017, it stood in for a forest in Belgium in DC's *Wonder Woman*.

Despite its popularity, applications to film here were suspended for a time due to sustainability concerns. But with filming on-site now back in action in this woodland, it won't be long until its verdant views grace our screens once more.

GLADIATOR (2000) ▶

The opening of Ridley Scott's epic—a grueling battle scene between Germanic peoples and Romans—was shot in the wood. The fires are real, as authorities had planned to clear part of the area *(p201)*.

CAPTAIN AMERICA: THE FIRST AVENGER (2011)

The heroic Captain America launched his first mission from an army base set amid the forest, returning there after rescuing Bucky and the other soldiers.

ROBIN HOOD (2010) ▶

Scott revisited the forest
for the filming of this famous
legend, with the pivotal siege
of Castle Chalus taking place
here. The castle was a set, built
by the production team.

WONDER WOMAN (2017)

While setting out to crash an
armistice gala at the German
High Command, the movie's
heroine and her team cut through
the (now Belgian) wood before
entering the castle *(p42)*.

2

FLIGHTS OF FANTASY

Tales of fantasy provide ample opportunity to shake off the demands of the everyday. To swoop on dragon-back over stunning desert sands. To fight fiendish creatures in gloomy forest glades. Perhaps even to slip through a rift in time to explore our planet before we mapped its every corner. Without these stories of monsters and magic, might the real world seem a little less colorful?

Fantasy might be escapist, but it needs to be convincing. The most spellbinding fantasy movies build their elaborate worlds through the meticulous choice of location, making even the most familiar locations seem enchanted. They weave their spells around places on earth that are already so awe-inspiring and ancient, so fantastical and foreign, that you'd be forgiven for thinking they'd been pieced together from actual footage of far-off lands.

GAME OF THRONES

Spread across an array of countries, *Game of Thrones'* eye-popping locations are so vital to the look and feel of the show, that they almost become characters in their own right.

YEAR
2011–2019

LOCATION
**ICELAND; CROATIA;
NORTHERN IRELAND;
SPAIN**

George R. R. Martin whose fantasy saga *A Song of Ice and Fire* was adapted for the TV show—once famously opined that his sprawling, battle-heavy masterpiece would be impossible to film. Thankfully, he was wrong. The show's titanic success is a result of the rich and layered storytelling; the use of state-of-the-art CGI; the actors' peerless performances; and, of course, untold units of blood, sweat, and tears. But fans would never have believed so deeply in the solidity of this strange yet familiar new world were it not for the real stars

of the show: the locations. Each of the show's four principal shooting locations—Iceland, Croatia, Spain, and Northern Ireland—captured and conveyed something essential about the continents of Westeros and Essos. The frozen, grand expanse of Iceland provided the perfect canvas for the echoing emptiness found north of The Wall. The historical treasure trove that is Croatia was the perfect fit for the treacherous city of King's Landing. The lush splendor of Spain breathed life and vibrancy into the cities of Highgarden and Meereen. And the

① Grjótagjá
This small lava cave, famous for its geothermal hot spring, was Jon Snow and Ygritte's secret hideaway in season 3. It's here Jon breaks his vow to the Night's Watch in episode 5.

② Svínafellsjökull
Gígjökull, Vatnajökull, and the enormous Svínafellsjökull glaciers all doubled for the frozen lands of the north.

⑤ Kirkjufell
Photogenic Kirkjufell had the perfect profile to become Arrowhead Mountain, an ominous landmark beyond The Wall.

④ Skógafoss
Jon takes Daenerys to Skógafoss waterfall when the pair are riding dragons around the north. A second level was added digitally.

③ Þjóðveldisbærinn Stöng
A recreation of a Viking farm lies in Þjórsárdalur valley. In season 4, it was viciously raided by Wildlings, who spare the life of a boy to send a message to Castle Black.

ICELAND

Húsavík · Hólmavík · Blönduós · Akureyri · ① Grjótagjá · Egilsstaðir · Reyðarfjörður · ⑤ Kirkjufell · *Langjökull* · Borgarnes · *Vatnajökull* · ③ Svínafellsjökull ② · Reykjavík · ③ Þjóðveldisbærinn Stöng · Skaftafell · Selfoss · Hvolsvöllur · ④ Skógafoss

DID YOU KNOW?

SOUND OF DRAGONS

To achieve the unique vocal stylings of an ice dragon, sound designer Paula Fairfield used the voices of drunk *Game of Thrones* fans.

BUDGET FURS

IKEA rugs were used for the furs worn by the Nights' Watch.

IRON THRONE

When the late British monarch Elizabeth II visited the set, she declined to sit on the Iron Throne. Rules of antiquity state that a monarch can't occupy the seat of power of another state or country.

weather-worn coasts of Northern Ireland were a fitting home for the Starks of Winterfell. Some would say that the series' location scouts did their jobs so well that it's impossible to imagine these fantastical places set anywhere else.

From season 2, King's Landing was filmed around Dubrovnik, Croatia. Prior to *Game of Thrones*, this walled city was most famous for its blend of Byzantine and Venetian influence, and its well-preserved medieval center. Nowadays, however, visitors are more likely to seek out the route of Cersei Lannister's memorable walk of shame than discover the city's maritime trading history. While the show's various set-dressings have all gone, the city—with its strong medieval walls and ancient streets—still looks remarkably

Gradac
Park
8

The Minčeta Tower, or House of the Undying, located on Dubrovnik's famous city walls

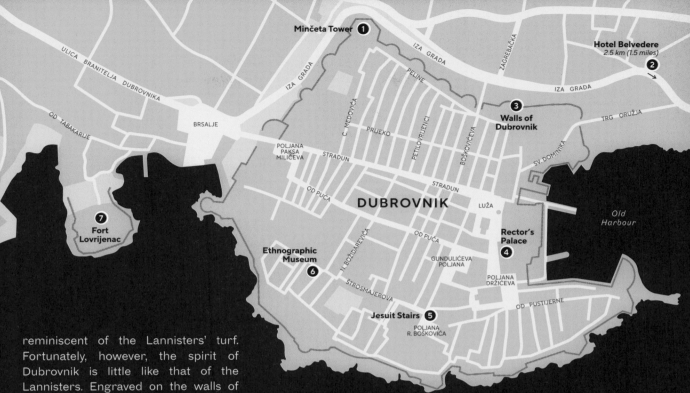

Minčeta Tower ①

ULICA BRANITELJA DUBROVNIKA

OD TABAKARIJE

BRSALJE

IZA GRADA

PELINE

IZA GRADA

ZAGREBAČKA

IZA GRADA

Hotel Belvedere ②
2.5 km (1.5 miles)

TRG ORUŽJA

Walls of Dubrovnik ③

SV. DOMINIKA

C. MEDOVIĆA

PRIJEKO

PETILOVRIJENCI

BOŠKOVIĆEVA

POLJANA
PAKSA
MILIĆEVA

STRADUN

OD PUČA

STRADUN

LUŽA

DUBROVNIK

*Old
Harbour*

**Fort
Lovrijenac** ⑦

N. BOŽIDAREVIĆA

OD PUČA

**Rector's
Palace** ④

**Ethnographic
Museum** ⑥

GUNDULIĆEVA
POLJANA

POLJANA
DRŽIĆEVA

ŠTROSMAJEROVA

OD PUSTIJERNE

Jesuit Stairs ⑤

POLJANA
R. BOŠKOVIĆA

---

reminiscent of the Lannisters' turf. Fortunately, however, the spirit of Dubrovnik is little like that of the Lannisters. Engraved on the walls of Fort Lovrijenac, to the west of the city—which doubles as the Red Keep, home of the Lannisters—is the inscription: "Freedom cannot be sold for all the gold." If only a certain *Game of Thrones* family had subscribed to that sentiment.

A production on the scale of *Game of Thrones* naturally necessitates the sort of logistical planning rarely seen outside of a military campaign. Northern Ireland alone reportedly played host to 12,986 extras. The statistics beyond the on-screen extras are just as startling. Over the show's eight-season run, the production team concocted a staggering 4,000 gallons of fake blood, burned through 20,900 candles, used some 20,000,000 screws and bolts, and scattered 52,000 bags of paper snow.

Despite all the jet-setting, the myriad moving parts, and the sheer scale and physicality of the production, accidents were kept to a minimum. Most of them were in fact weather related. You would be forgiven for imagining that those

---

① **Minčeta Tower**
Daenerys frantically searches for her stolen dragons in Qarth's House of the Undying (the imposing Minčeta Tower).

② **Hotel Belvedere**
The Mountain fights Prince Martell with eye-watering results on the amphitheater-style patio of this abandoned hotel.

③

Walls of Dubrovnik
The cast spent hours across various episodes walking and plotting along these 13th-century walls.

④ **Rector's Palace**
Daenerys attempts to source ships from the Spice King on the atrium stairs of this Gothic palace.

⑤ **Jesuit Stairs**
Cersei Lannister endures her walk of shame on the Baroque Jesuit Stairs in season 5.

⑥ **Ethnographic Museum**
Housed inside a spacious 16th-century granary, this museum became Littlefinger's brothel.

⑦ **Fort Lovrijenac**
High on a rocky outcrop, this fort (with some CGI additions) played the Red Keep, home of the Lannisters.

⑧

Gradac Park
The Purple Wedding and subsequent poisoning of King Joffrey took place at this quiet park.

brushes with death occurred in the dark, subzero climes of Iceland or in the tinder-dry summer scrublands of Spain, but it was actually Northern Ireland that provided two of the show's biggest behind-the-scenes weather scares. In 2011, the tail end of Hurricane Katia assaulted the coast near the Northern Irish village of Ballintoy, the town whose harbor doubles as much of the Iron Islands. After whipping up waves, it howled inland, scooping up a marquee with a handful of the show's crew and extras inside. Despite the shock, only five people were injured, none of them seriously.

Nature upped its game for season 6, when part of the rainy Magheramorne Quarry that housed the set for Castle Black started to crumble, sending rocks and boulders (some of them, according to one eyewitness, the size of London

Northern Ireland's atmospheric Dark Hedges

town houses) tumbling down to the ground. Mercifully, no one was injured. The Wall at Castle Black would remain standing, at least until the hulking ice dragon Viserion destroyed it.

Security on set, however, wasn't just about safety. As the show became more popular, keeping spoilers out of the public domain became a full-time job. Extras working on the show had to sign strict nondisclosure agreements and faced financial penalties for breaking them. Sometimes, the use of blocking screens and perimeter patrols weren't enough to deter zealous fans from invading the set—especially once the more enthusiastic among them started deploying drones. The production team was eventually forced to enter into a spoiler-themed arms race, using special electronic equipment to shoot drones from the sky.

But you needn't worry about all of that. Now that our watch (of *Game of Thrones*) has ended, the veil of secrecy around the show's locations has lifted, and Westeros—every beautiful corner of it—is all yours to explore.

① **Ballintoy Harbour**
This tiny harbor and its surrounding inlets and beaches was the port of Pyke on the Iron Islands.

② **The Dark Hedges**
Arya travels in disguise under the twisted beech trees lining the Kings Road in the first episode of season 2.

③

Cushendun Caves
Melisandre gives birth to a shadow assassin here during season 2.

④ **Castle Ward**
This 18th-century castle was used for several locations, but it most famously played Winterfell, the home of the Starks.

A Coruña
Santander
Gaztelugatxe ⑥
Bayonne
FRANCE
Toulouse
Bilbao
León
Pamplona
Perpignan
Porto
Valladolid
Zaragoza
Girona ⑦
Barcelona
SPAIN
Madrid
Cuenca
⑨ Castillo de Zafra
PORTUGAL
Salamanca
⑧ Peñíscola
Cáceres
⑭ Trujillo Alcazaba
Valencia
Lisbon
Ciudad Real
Itálica ⑬
⑪ Castillo de Almodóvar
Cartagena
⑫ Seville
Faro
Tabernas ⑩
Málaga
Almería

⑤ Game of Thrones Studio Tour
This popular studio tour features recreations of the series's sets, original props, and costumes.

Gaztelugatxe
Snaking through the Bay of Biscay to reach this islet are the steps leading to the (digitally rendered) Dragonstone Castle.

⑦ Girona
Arya trains to become a Faceless in Braavos, which was depicted by the ancient Catalonian city of Girona. The city's hulking cathedral later appears as the fated Great Sept of Baelor in King's Landing.

⑧ Peñíscola
The ancient coastal city of Peñíscola was cast as Meereen in season 6.

Castillo de Zafra
Sat upon a rocky outcrop in Guadalajara, this castle was the Tower of Joy, the birthplace of Jon Snow.

⑩ Tabernas
Season 6 sees Daenerys leading the Dothraki into the deserts here. Vaes Dothrak, the Dothraki capital, was set around nearby Pechina.

⑪ Castillo de Almodóvar
This beautiful castle is Highgarden, the home of Olenna Tyrell.

⑫ Seville
Seville's stunning Real Alcázar played House Martell's dazzling Dorne Palace.

⑬ Itálica
The Roman ruins of Itálica, in Santiponce, appear as the Dragonpit twice—first when Cersei and Daenerys meet and again when judgment is passed on Jon Snow.

Trujillo Alcazaba
This huge Moorish fort in Cáceres became Tywin Lannister's stone stronghold of Casterly Rock. It is attacked by Daenerys's army of the Unsullied in the third episode of season 7.

🎞 HOUSE OF THE DRAGON

Game of Thrones' prequel series—which focuses on the troubled reign of House Targaryen—shot primarily in the UK and Spain.

ST. MICHAEL'S MOUNT
This tidal island and castle in Cornwall, UK, became the House of Velaryon's High Tide on Driftmark. It's where Rhaenyra Targaryen and King Viserys travel to meet a potential suitor.

CÁCERES
This UNESCO World Heritage Site in Spain was the perfect fit for an earlier King's Landing. Nearby Trujillo—used as Casterly Rock in *Game of Thrones*—was also used for exteriors.

CASTILLO DE LA CALAHORRA
Granada's 14th-century Castillo de la Calahorra masquerades as Pentos, home to House Targaryen. The building is thought to have been a prison during the Spanish Reconquest of Moorish Spain.

OUTLANDER

This swashbuckling saga, adapted from Diana Gabaldon's bestselling books, uses Scotland's rugged scenery to stunning effect, bringing to life the country's past in places both real and imagined.

YEAR
2014–

LOCATION
SCOTLAND

On the world stage, Scotland doesn't always get to be the star of its own show. Even the historical biopic *Braveheart* was filmed predominantly in Ireland. Thankfully, the TV series *Outlander* redresses this balance by keeping Scotland's beautiful highland vistas and mist-shrouded lochs at the front and center of its proudly Scottish period romance.

Outlander's time-traveling adventures begin in 1945 when army nurse Claire Randall is whisked back in time to 1743; here, she falls in love with rebel Highlander Jamie Fraser. The first season follows the pair on adventures around Jacobite Scotland, shining the spotlight on the country's gorgeous scenery—from the wild hills outside the village of Kinloch Rannoch (where the standing stones are set) to the grand Blackness Castle, fortress of the villainous "Black Jack" Randall.

Later, Scotland gives the world a taste of its own medicine by standing in for France and the US. Fife's Dysart harbor becomes the port town of Le Havre; Hopetoun House in West Lothian serves as the streets of Paris; and Drummond Castle Gardens in Perthshire does some heavy lifting as Versailles. Claire and Jamie's North Carolina settlement, meanwhile, was filmed in the woods of Doune. Some scenes were shot outside of Scotland— both Prague and Cape Town appear in season 2—but production for the series was largely based in and around the Wardpark Film & Television Studios in Cumbernauld, central Scotland.

Scotland's vast lochs and country homes continue to be the foundation for the show's storylines. The country's compact size makes it easy for fans to undertake a pilgrimage of *Outlander's*

Blackness Castle, where Jamie is held captive by "Black Jack" Randall

locations—and many have done just that. The so-called Outlander Effect (location tourism spawned by the show) has been responsible for a huge influx of tourists to the country, with most international visitors hailing from the US. In fact, Americans have embraced *Outlander* so enthusiastically that the National Trust for Scotland's Foundation USA receives hundreds of thousands of dollars on a regular basis, donated by fans to ensure the full maintenance of the properties that appear in the show. Such is the power of the Outlander Effect that it's rumoured that, in 2014, then UK Prime Minister David Cameron requested that Sony executives delay the eagerly anticipated release of *Outlander* in the UK, fearing the show's British debut could influence the upcoming referendum on Scottish independence. Not bad for a romantic swashbuckling saga.

Doune Castle

Doune Castle was used as Castle Leoch. It previously appeared in *Monty Python and the Holy Grail*.

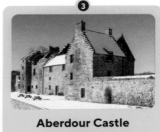

Aberdour Castle

Claire and Murtagh take Jamie to recover in the Benedictine monastery, played by Aberdour Castle, after his prison ordeal.

Kinloch Rannoch

Craigh na Dun, where the stone circle used by Claire was set, was filmed around Kinloch Rannoch. The stones don't exist in real life, however.

Blackness Castle

This coastal fortress plays the headquarters of "Black Jack" Randall. Claire and Jamie leap into the sea from here to escape.

Pollok Country Park

The grounds of Castle Leoch were shot in Pollok Country Park. The park, located just outside Glasgow, also appeared as the French countryside in some scenes in season 2.

SCOTLAND

Loch Ness
Aviemore
Aberdeen
Balmoral
Stonehaven
Fort William
Grampian Mountains
Kinloch Rannoch ❶
Pitlochry
Dundee
Crianlarich
Perth
St Andrews
Inveraray
Doune Castle ❷
Stirling
❸ Aberdour Castle
Blackness Castle ❹
❺ Edinburgh
Glasgow
❻ Linlithgow Palace
Hopetoun House
Pollok Country Park ❼
Peebles
Selkirk
Irvine
Jedburgh
Ayr
Dumfries
Carlisle
ENGLAND

Linlithgow Palace

Jamie was imprisoned and sentenced to hang in Wentworth Prison, in reality the grand Linlithgow Palace.

Hopetoun House

Hawkins Estate, the stately home of the antagonist Duke of Sandringham, was filmed in Hopetoun House.

UPSTAIRS, DOWNSTAIRS

From quintessential stately homes in the UK to castles in Japan, historic buildings are regularly brought back to grand and glamorous life on-screen.

VERSAILLES, FRANCE

Whether in *Midnight in Paris* (2011) or *Marie Antoinette* (2006), scenes shot in the Palace of Versailles always look opulent. Not only is it costly to film inside this historical monument, but there are strict rules, too. For example, *Marie Antoinette* had to be filmed over-night, and use of the furniture and window shutters was forbidden.

HIGHCLERE CASTLE, UK

This stately British manor is best known as the home of the Crawley family in *Downton Abbey* (2010–2015). Movie buffs, however, will be quick to note that it was also where Stanley Kubrick shot one of *Eyes Wide Shut*'s (1999) most intimate scenes.

OSAKA CASTLE, JAPAN

Though it stands at nearly 200 ft (60 m) tall, this 16th-century castle often looks smaller on-screen. It might be down to the fact that so many *kaiju* movies have been shot here, with the genre's giant monsters battling next to it, like in *Godzilla Raids Again* (1955). For this sequel movie, a miniature was used to achieve the castle's destruction.

CASTLE HOWARD, UK

A lavish North Yorkshire mansion, this site has lent aristocratic authenticity to projects as wide-ranging as *Brideshead Revisited* (in both the 1981 and 2008 versions), the steamy drama *Bridgerton* (2019–), and *Garfield: A Tale of Two Kitties* (2006). As with Versailles, there are restrictions on filming in place, especially around the building's delicate artwork.

DOVER CASTLE, UK

There's hardly a recent movie in which this striking medieval castle hasn't cropped up at one point or another. One of the more exhilarating scenes that was shot here can be seen in *Avengers: Age of Ultron* (2015), in which it doubled for a Hydra outpost.

NEUSCHWANSTEIN CASTLE, GERMANY

This picturesque German castle appears in a number of classics—the eye-catching towers are featured in both *The Great Escape* (1963) and *Chitty Chitty Bang Bang* (1968). It was also the supposed inspiration for the castle in Walt Disney's *Sleeping Beauty* (1959).

1 The Hall of Mirrors in the Palace of Versailles

2 Highclere Castle, the fictional Crawleys' home

3 Osaka Castle, a 20th-century reconstruction of a 16th-century landmark

4 A scene from the 1981 *Brideshead Revisited,* at Castle Howard

5 Dover Castle, an outpost of Hydra

6 The elaborate Neuschwanstein Castle

1

2

3

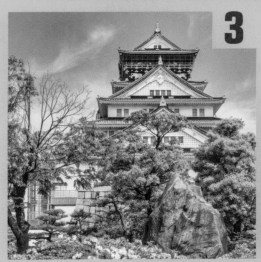

4

5

6

THE PRINCESS BRIDE

The romantic, pastoral countryside of England and Ireland provides a picturesque background for this self-aware fairy-tale love story, based on the classic novel.

YEAR
1987

LOCATION
ENGLAND; IRELAND

To adapt William Goldman's book *The Princess Bride,* director Rob Reiner (a huge fan of the book) headed to the English countryside. The pastoral landscape here looked little changed from medieval times (the era in which the book is set), and rural Derbyshire in particular had all the rolling green hills and scenic valleys he envisioned for the world of Florin.

While most of the filming took place in England, Ireland's Cliffs of Moher had their moment as the Cliffs of Insanity. It's here that the thrilling sword fight takes place—though most of the battle was shot on set at Shepperton Studios. Cary Elwes (Westley) and Mandy Patinkin (Inigo Montoya) practiced for months to bring the scene to life, sparring whenever they had free time. Elwes may have been slick with the sword, but he had less luck elsewhere. He broke his toe joy riding on André the Giant's quad bike and hid it from Reiner (spot the limp in the film). He was also knocked out by co-star Christopher Guest during the forest kidnapping scene—by accident.

But you don't have to risk life and limb to experience Reiner's beloved picture-book fantasy. Just whisper "as you wish" into the wind as you wander across the verdant hills of Derbyshire, and let your imagination do the rest.

❶ Cave Dale
After a bitter argument, Buttercup pushes Dread Pirate Roberts down this valley and his true identity, as her beloved farm boy Westley, is revealed.

❷ Haddon Hall
The Florin scenes were shot at this country house, a regular location for Jane Austen adaptations.

❹ Lathkill Dale
The Battle of Wits, in which Westley tricks the evil Vizzini, was filmed here.

❸ Robin Hood's Stride
This boulder-strewn area was the site of the battle between Fezzik and Westley.

Castleton

Cave Dale ❶

Bradwell

Hathersage

Dronfield

DERBYSHIRE

Buxton

River Derwent

Baslow

Bakewell

Lathkill Dale ❹

❷ Haddon Hall

Robin Hood's Stride ❸

Darley Dale

River Dove

Matlock

THE WITCHER

The monster-hunting world of *The Witcher* infiltrated Europe's breathtaking castles and natural landscapes—but a good dose of visual effects was needed to bring this thrilling fantasy to life.

YEAR
2019–

LOCATION
WORLDWIDE

While *The Witcher's* twisted fairy-tale aesthetics were largely a testament to the show's VFX crews, the series owes a lot to Central Europe's castles, too.

The first season of *The Witcher* was largely shot in Hungary and the Canary Islands, but it was Poland's mighty Ogrodzieniec Castle that formed the backdrop for the finale's climactic Battle of Sodden Hill. CGI was used to place a chasm and bridge over the villages at its foothills, intensifying the sense of dread, but the castle itself looks just as formidable in real life as it does on screen. Elsewhere in Europe, Austria's impressive Kreuzenstein Castle was digitally aged to become the abandoned castle of Temeria. CGI wasn't always necessary, however. To transform the inner courtyard of Budapest's strikingly medieval-looking Vajdahunyad Castle (actually only built in 1896) into the residence of Stregobor the wizard, all the production team needed were a few plants, props, and additional lighting.

Spain's beautiful Canary Islands also played a key role in *The Witcher's* first season, in particular Gran Canaria. In episode 4, the sandy plains of Dunas de Maspalomas appear when Yennefer and Queen Kalis of Lyria frantically flee from an assassin through multiple portals. In the same episode, Yennefer later ends up on the dramatic black sands of

Poland's ruined Ogrodzieniec Castle, the setting for the pivotal Battle of Sodden Hill

Playa de Guayedra, a wild beach on the north side of the island.

While the second season was shot mostly in the UK, the third promised a return to international locations, with scenes filmed in Croatia, Slovenia, and Morocco. *The Witcher* might have required a dose of technical wizardry to bring the world of Geralt of Rivia to life, but it isn't hard to imagine these real-world settings crawling with mutants and monsters.

THE LORD OF THE RINGS

Hobbit habitats, elven woodland dwellings, and Mordor's ashen plains seemed to already exist in New Zealand; all director Peter Jackson had to do was bring them to life.

YEAR
2001, 2002, 2003

LOCATION
NEW ZEALAND

The conical Mount Ngāuruhoe (aka Mount Doom), Tongariro National Park

Peter Jackson didn't have to look far when scouting locations for *The Lord of the Rings* trilogy. The director's home of New Zealand had it all. Rolling green hills became the ideal home for little hobbits; snow-dusted mountains loomed over the landscape just like Mount Doom; vast, sweeping plains provided the perfect backdrop for epic battles; and mossy, sun-dappled forests looked fit for an elf already. Across New Zealand's two beautiful islands, Jackson found more than 150 backdrops to storyboard the end of Middle Earth's Third Age, and later, his prequel movie series *The Hobbit*.

Jackson's production lasted far longer than Frodo and Sam's quest to Mordor, but everything started in the same, humble place: The Shire™. The film's production team began transforming a local sheep farm in Waikato, on the

PUTTING NZ ON THE MAP

Peter Jackson's movie series did wonders for New Zealand's tourism industry. According to Tourism New Zealand, nearly one in five visitors first discovered this dazzling country through *The Lord of the Rings* series.

North Island, into this idyllic spot in 1999. (The same site is now the Hobbiton™ Movie Set.) From here, Jackson and his crew traveled the length and breadth of New Zealand, filming in some of the

Samwise Gamgee's home, complete with a mailbox, at the popular Hobbiton™ Movie Set

country's most incredible landscapes. In the first filmed scene, the hobbits hide from Ringwraiths in Mount Victoria's dense woodland around Wellington; just north of here, enchanting Kaitoke Regional Park became the elf haven of Rivendell. Meanwhile on the scenic South Island, the forest realm of Lothlórien was, fittingly, shot in a place called Paradise *(p64)*.

Blessed with New Zealand's natural bounty, Jackson required fewer add-ons than you might think to recreate Tolkien's magical Middle Earth. The Putangirua Pinnacles Scenic Reserve, for example, looks just as eerie as it does when Aragorn, Legolas, and Gimli stir the Army of the Dead—minus any vengeful ghosts. Meanwhile, the sacred Mount Ngāuruhoe—once the country's most active volcano—really is perfectly conical in shape like Mount Doom.

PETER JACKSON IN NEW ZEALAND

The director's birthplace is featured in even more of his movies.

BRAINDEAD
(1992)

Jackson's zombie comedy slasher *Braindead* is a cult classic among gore fans. Scenes were shot at Wellington Zoo and the Putangirua Pinnacles.

KING KONG
(2005)

The monster movie saw the Wellington suburb of Lyall Bay become Skull Island, with a large-scale set built at nearby Shelly Bay. Aragorn actor Viggo Mortensen also learned to surf here during *The Lord of the Rings*.

THE HOBBIT
(2012)

New Zealand takes center stage in *The Hobbit* movie series. Bilbo's eagle getaway takes place in Fiordland National Park, while Laketown is set on the real-life Lake Pukaki.

The striking Kawarau River Canyon, where the Pillars of the Kings were added

However, the sheer scale of Jackson's production inevitably required some set-building. The medieval-inspired city of Edoras was custom built on craggy Mount Sunday and a huge sound stage was created in Dry Creek Quarry for the Battle of Helm's Deep; this was later repurposed for the city of Minas Tirith. Bigatures (huge miniature models) were also used to create places like Rivendell— these were all made by the New Zealand–based special effects company Wētā Workshop.

Jackson made a habit of employing fellow Kiwis. His mammoth project needed thousands of people to make up the on-screen armies, after all. For the Battle of Helm's Deep, scores of extras were recruited to play the Uruk Hai; after 120 rainy days (well, mostly nights)

of shoots, they all received a T-shirt with the slogan "I survived Helm's Deep." For the Uruk Hai's battle cries, the production crew recorded the clamorous sounds of 25,000 cricket fans in a local stadium. The New Zealand Army was also called up to help, assisting with the building of The Shire™ and playing extras for the Battle of the Black Gate (shot in the Rangipo Desert).

The details of Jackson's production are impressive to say the least, but it's the equally impressive locations that remain today. Returning to New Zealand to shoot *The Hobbit*, the director added even more of the country's beautiful locations to movie-lovers' bucket lists. Many of these are little changed and just as fantastical as ever—as if dreamed up by Tolkien himself.

⑨ Kawarau River Canyon

The enormous stone statues of Isildur and his father Elendil, known as the Pillars of the Kings, were added digitally to the Kawarau River Canyon cliffs.

① Hobbiton™ Movie Set

The pretty, pastoral Shire™ was partially demolished after *The Lord of the Rings* wrapped. It was later rebuilt and extended for *The Hobbit* series and it's now a popular tourist attraction on the North Island.

Tawhai and Mangawhero Falls

Two waterfalls near the base of Mount Ngāuruhoe were used to film the capture of Gollum by Faramir in *The Two Towers*.

⑧ Mount Sunday

Rohan capital Edoras was built on Mount Sunday, a rocky outcrop surrounded by mountains. The town has gone but the scenery remains the same.

② Mount Ngāuruhoe

The beautifully symmetrical Mount Ngāuruhoe, in Tongariro National Park, stands in for Mount Doom. The mountain is a sacred site and climbing is discouraged.

④ Kaitoke Regional Park

This gorgeous, sun-dappled park became the elven home of Rivendell. A replica gate has been built and information boards help identify where scenes were shot.

⑦ Mount Owen

The Fellowship—minus Gandalf—flee to this mountain after escaping the Mines of Moria.

⑤ Wētā Cave

This free museum features movie memorabilia and prop replicas from the Wētā Workshop team, who produced many of the special effects and miniature models for the movie series.

⑥ Putangirua Pinnacles

These extraordinary rock formations formed the dreaded Dimholt Road that Aragorn, Gimli, and Legolas trek to wake the Army of the Dead.

Map labels:

Te Kao
Kaitaia
Whangarei
Warkworth
Auckland
Pokeno
Hamilton
Tauranga
① Hobbiton™ Movie Set
North Island
Rotorua
Opotiki
New Plymouth
Taupo
Mount Ngāuruhoe ②
Turangi
Tawhai and ③
Mangawhero Falls
Gisborne
Waiouru
Whanganui
Kaitoke Regional Park ④
Palmerston North
NEW ZEALAND
Tasman Sea
Takaka
Nelson
Picton
Mount Owen ⑦
Westport
Wellington
Wētā Cave ⑤
Putangirua Pinnacles ⑥
Greymouth
Kaikoura
Pacific Ocean
South Island
Christchurch
Mount Sunday ⑧
Geraldine
Akaroa
Queenstown
Kawarau River Canyon ⑨
Oamaru
Te Anau
Invercargill

THE FELLOWSHIP OF THE RING (2001) ▶

The forests of Paradise are featured in the heartbreaking scene that sees Boromir killed by multiple arrows to the chest during a Uruk-hai attack.

X-MEN ORIGINS: WOLVERINE (2009)

Following his escape from the facility that gave him an adamantium skeleton, Logan is taken in by an elderly couple and hides out in their farmhouse here.

PARADISE

Looking for Paradise? It's right here on earth. Made up of ethereal mossy forests and rolling green pastures, this verdant valley frequently steals the scenes.

While it may not be as well known as go-to locations like, say, Monument Valley *(p134)*, this paradisaical spot packs a punch when it comes to movie magic. Nestled amid the soaring peaks of the Southern Alps, Paradise is most famous for its roles in *The Lord of the Rings* franchise *(p60)*. The valley's beech woods stood in for the forest of Lothlórien in *The Fellowship of the Ring* (2001), while in *The Hobbit: Desolation of Smaug* (2013), one of its high-country farms was the setting for Beorn's House. Beyond Middle Earth, Paradise and its surrounds have featured in big-budget blockbuster *The Lion, the Witch and the Wardrobe* (2005) and TV drama *Top of the Lake* (2013–17).

Getting to Paradise isn't easy. It's a 45-minute drive from Queenstown to the tiny town of Glenorchy, followed by a further 25 minutes along a narrow gravel track. But that doesn't seem to put off film crews, who keep coming back, time and again, to this remote pocket of paradise.

THE LION, THE WITCH AND THE WARDROBE (2005) ▶

As the White Witch's power wanes and Narnia is released from its perpetual winter, the Pevensie children stroll through the valley's lush landscape.

TOP OF THE LAKE (2013–2017)

Many of the scenes featuring Laketop—the main town in this award-winning dark mystery drama—were filmed close to Paradise in nearby Glenorchy.

SUPERNATURAL

Sam and Dean Winchester faced numerous demons on their 15-year road trip across America, though most of the destinations they visited were actually north of the border in Canada.

YEAR
2005–2020

LOCATION
VANCOUVER, CANADA

Rolling for a record-breaking 327 episodes, the paranormal epic *Supernatural* remains the longest-running sci-fi/fantasy series in US TV history. Over the course of the show, the Winchester brothers spent 15 years driving across America in their Chevrolet Impala, hunting down things that go bump in the night. Fun fact: the car may be iconic now, but creator Eric Kripke originally wanted elder brother Dean Winchester to drive a 1965 Ford Mustang. It was one of his neighbors who pointed out that "it has to be a '67 Impala because you can put a body in the trunk."

Early in *Supernatural*'s development, Kripke envisioned the series as an anthology show before settling on a horror-tinged version of the American road trip. Although the prospect of exploring a new place every week is exciting for viewers, a show that's constantly on the move faces significant challenges in the budget department. Luckily, in Vancouver and its surrounds, *Supernatural*'s production team found everything they needed for a country-wide tour. The Canadian city became the show's promised land, an area so versatile that it was the Winchesters' base of operations from beginning to end—with the exception of the Los Angeles–based pilot.

Along the way, Vancouver was trans-formed into American cities, some real (San Francisco, St. Louis, Sioux Falls), others entirely fictional (like Kripke's Hollow, which was humorously named after the show's creator). Perhaps most remarkable is the way *Supernatural*'s production designers used the region as a vast TV studio, molding real-life places to fit the needs of the story arc

The Canadian city of Vancouver, *Supernatural*'s base of operations

① Spur 4 Bridge

Spur 4 Bridge
The last scene of the series was filmed at Spur 4 Bridge near the Mid-Valley Viewpoint.

② Buntzen Lake

Buntzen Lake
Buntzen Lake featured as Lake Manitoc during season 1's "Dead in the Water" episode.

Burrard Inlet
The entrance to the Men of Letters Bunker is on the south side of the Burrard Inlet under the Ironworkers Memorial Bridge.

VanDusen Botanical Garden
This lush garden became the LaVeau art gallery in the season 13 episode "Funeralia."

Riverview Hospital
Riverview Hospital was used to portray several locations throughout the series, including a prison and various apartments and hospitals.

Burger Heaven
This New Westminster spot was the location of an interview during the season 8 episode "Southern Comfort."

Ladner Harbour Park
Appearing in seasons 9 to 13, the gateway to Heaven was a simple sandbox in Ladner Harbour Park.

North 40 Park Reserve
Roads crossing North 40 Park Reserve were used for a number of sets, including Harvelle's Roadhouse.

n fact, popular buildings such as the spectacularly spooky Riverview Hospital (which starred in series such as *The X-Files*, *Riverdale,* and *Battlestar Galactica*) were dressed and redressed to portray multiple locations in the show.

Trips to the great beyond were also a major part of the *Supernatural* mix, with the entrance to Heaven inevitably filmed on the outskirts of Vancouver. You'll find this glorious gateway in an unassuming sandbox in Ladner Harbour Park—and that's got to be one for the tourist brochures.

PAN'S LABYRINTH

Guillermo del Toro's twisted tale may veer into the world of fantasy—
with all its fairies, fauns, and fiendish monsters—but its reality is
rooted in Spain's war-stricken past.

YEAR
2006

LOCATION
SPAIN

A Gothic fairy tale, *Pan's Labyrinth* was so good it made the king of horror, Stephen King, "squirm." (Director Guillermo del Toro was obviously delighted.) But strip away the fantasy and the undeniably creepy monsters (partly inspired by Francisco Goya paintings) and *Pan's Labyrinth* reveals itself as a story of war.

The movie is set in 1944, at the end of Spain's Civil War, and del Toro's location choices aptly reflect this period of history. In the opening scene, viewers glimpse the crumbling ruins of Belchite, a Spanish village that was destroyed during the war and left as a memorial. This historical site aptly foreshadows the trauma that later seems to infect every building, plant, and creature in del Toro's tale.

The majority of the movie, however, was shot around the Scots pine forests of the Sierra de Guadarrama, where fighting took place during the war. While filming here was difficult—it was experiencing its worst drought in 30 years—historical accuracy was key. The further del Toro embedded his story in reality, the more fantastical the fantasy became.

The ruins of Belchite,
a village destroyed
during the Spanish
Civil War

1 **Indian Beach**

Indian Beach

Jacob tells Bella about the area's local legends on a walk along La Push beach. This was filmed on the boulder-strewn Indian Beach in Ecola State Park.

2 **The Shire**

The Multnomah Falls are seen in the background of the baseball scene. The game itself takes place in The Shire, a field owned by the University of Oregon.

3 **Carver Café**

Bella and Charlie have dinner at this low-key, local café, which still serves great burgers.

4 **Silver Falls State Park**

Silver Falls State Park

Walk beneath the trees Edward and "spider monkey" Bella fly through in this state park. The opening deer-chase scene was filmed here, too.

TWILIGHT

The overcast skies and damp, dense forests of Oregon made for the perfect setting, and ideal hideout, for the moody vampires in this blockbuster teen romance.

YEAR
2008

LOCATION
OREGON, US

After another studio's failed attempt to adapt Stephanie Meyer's popular teen-vampire tale *Twilight*—which would have featured couple Bella and Edward fleeing the FBI on jet skis—Summit Pictures and indie director Catherine Hardwicke stepped in to translate the bestselling books to the big screen.

While there were no more high-speed chases from the law in this version, Edward Cullen and his vampire family still had issues—they couldn't be seen in the sun, lest they reveal their sparkling skin. In Meyer's book, the group settle in Forks, Washington. Hardwicke chose to film in rainy St. Helens, Oregon, instead, but Forks still found fame. The town saw a huge influx of fan tourism (despite no scenes being shot there) and embraced its association with the movie. There's even a parking spot reserved for Dr. Carlisle Cullen at the hospital.

While based in St. Helens, *Twilight* took full advantage of Oregon's surrounding scenery. The state's wild beaches, misty forests, and thundery skies mirrored the whirlwind drama of a teen romance—and Hardwicke's blue-green filter only added to the movie's brooding tone. Yet while Oregon was suitably rainy, bad weather wasn't always guaranteed. The baseball scene had to be shot in the chilly winter to ensure an overcast sky.

Although *Twilight* became a sensation, Hardwicke's vision was disregarded for the sequels, all of which were filmed in Canada. Only the original *Twilight* was shot in Oregon, but the Pacific Northwest still remains ground zero for vampires.

GOOD OMENS

Good Omens was once considered unfilmable, but by staying faithful to the story's British origins, this big-budget adaptation proved to be a slice of TV heaven … and hell.

The idyllic village of Hambleden, an ideal setting for Tadfield, the home of the Antichrist

Berwick St.

Aziraphale's bookstore was built on a set at RAF Bovingdon, but Neil Gaiman has said its location is probably this street.

① Berwick St.

② Sky Garden

③ Shakespeare's Globe

⑤ St. James's Park

④ Battersea Park Bandstand

Sky Garden

London's leafy retreat was recreated digitally to become Heaven, with views of famous landmarks like the Eiffel Tower.

St. James's Park

A bench on the north side of the lake in St. James's Park is a regular meeting place for everyone's favorite angel and demon duo.

Shakespeare's Globe

During episode 3's flashback sequence, Crowley and Aziraphale watch a poorly attended performance of *Hamlet* at Shakespeare's Globe theater. Here, they meet the famous playwright himself.

Battersea Park Bandstand

Aziraphale and Crowley have one of their many disagreements at the Battersea Park Bandstand.

YEAR
2019–

LOCATION
**ENGLAND;
SOUTH AFRICA**

Terry Pratchett and Neil Gaiman's beloved comic novel—about an angel and a demon teaming up to save the world from the Antichrist—nearly became a movie in the early 2000s. Luckily for fans, the movie didn't go through and the more suitable small screen (with its long-form storytelling) became home for the authors' labyrinthine take on the apocalypse. The duo's pact that they'd work only on *Good Omens*–related matters together appeared to put a permanent kibosh on the adaptation, however, when Pratchett died in 2015. Gaiman later revealed that before Pratchett passed away he had given him permission to write the script himself: *Good Omens* had a TV future.

Taking on showrunner duties, Gaiman was passionate about ensuring everything on screen was in tune with the pair's original vision. The resulting six-part series had genuinely Hollywood proportions yet never lost sight of its roots in southeast England.

Aziraphale and Crowley, the quirky representatives of Heaven and Hell, meet regularly in real-life parks, pubs, and restaurants all over London. Meanwhile, the thatched roofs and red telephone boxes of Hambleden, near Henley-on-Thames, made it an ideal stand-in for the quintessential English village of Tadfield (home of preteen Antichrist Adam Young).

For sequences where the scenery in the UK didn't quite fit the bill, the team flew out to South Africa. Pivotal scenes from the beginning of time were filmed across the amazing landscapes here—even though Cape Town's worst drought in decades meant the Garden of Eden's waterfall had to be digitally enhanced. Biblical Armageddon was ultimately averted, so plenty of *Good Omen* locations were still in one piece when cameras started rolling on the second season in 2021.

3

As we haven't quite harnessed the power of Doc and Marty McFly's time machine, movies might just be the closest we get to traveling back in time. It takes just one, endlessly quotable one-liner ("You're a wizard, Harry"), or the very first notes of a memorable soundtrack ("Who ya gonna call?"), and we're right back there with the family, gathered around the TV on a Saturday evening. Yes, watch *Jurassic Park* now and you're acutely aware that the dinosaurs aren't real—but don't you still feel a shiver down the spine at the first ripple of water?

Featuring some of our greatest heroes (the bumbling Jack Sparrow and the ever-polite Paddington Bear) and most iconic moments (it's hard to forget that first time-hopping journey in the DeLorean), these flicks are handed down from one generation to the next, reminding us all why we fell in love with the magic of movies in the first place.

HARRY POTTER

While J. K. Rowling's magical saga is now a worldwide phenomenon, when it came to transforming the books into films, production kept to Great Britain, putting the spotlight on its stunning locations and legions of talented actors.

YEAR
2001, 2002, 2004,
2005, 2007, 2009,
2010, 2011

LOCATION
ENGLAND;
SCOTLAND; WALES

The spellbinding world of *Harry Potter* has captured the hearts of generations, amassing scores of loyal fans around the world. With thousands lining up at midnight for the next installment, it was only a matter of time before the magic of J. K. Rowling's stories hit the big screen. Though the blockbuster adaptations of the best-selling novels were bankrolled by US studio Warner Bros., British producer David Heyman (who'd go on to produce the *Paddington [p80]* movies) ensured that the movie series never lost sight of its roots. That meant an almost exclusively British and Irish cast and an entirely UK-based production.

As well as filming in London studios, the *Harry Potter* series made extensive use of real-life locations around the British Isles to tell its tale of "the boy who lived." A full pilgrimage to the wizarding world, then, requires plenty of travel—and for Muggles, apparition is sadly not an option. For most fans, there is no better place to start than at London's King's Cross, the home of platform 9¾. This station makes the most of its

wizarding associations with a platform 9¾ exhibit and a Potter-themed gift shop. Chances of hitching a ride on the *Hogwarts Express* from here are slim, however; the *Express* was played by the *Jacobite* steam train that runs from Fort William in Scotland and crosses the scenic Glenfinnan Viaduct, as featured in the movies, on its way to Mallaig.

If you were to board the *Hogwarts Express*, you'd reach Hogwarts School of Witchcraft and Wizardry. Harry's famous alma mater was an amalgam of locations, with producers taking

The popular recreation of Platform 9¾ at London's King's Cross station

The Jacobite steam train (or the *Hogwarts Express* to fans) traveling across the Glenfinnan Viaduct

WIZARDING WORLDS ON SCREEN

Witches and wizards may be magical beings but more often than not their worlds are very much based on Earth, or at least filmed there.

HOCUS POCUS
(1993)

Numerous scenes in this wicked family flick were shot in historic Salem. You'll find Thackery Binx's house in the Pioneer Village, a living history museum in the city.

STARDUST
(2007)

Filming for this fantasy romance took place all around the UK. Charming Castle Combe played the fictional village of Wall, while the Isle of Skye stood in for the kingdom of Stormhold.

FANTASTIC BEASTS AND WHERE TO FIND THEM
(2016)

For its New York–set scenes, this prequel *Potter* series filmed in historical buildings around Liverpool. The rally was shot at St. George's Hall

Christ Church college's dining room, which inspired Hogwarts's Great Hall

inspiration from a plethora of historic buildings. Despite Rowling saying that she imagined Hogwarts in Scotland, most of Harry's school was shot south of the border in England. In the first two movies, Northumberland's Alnwick Castle played Hogwarts's exteriors (scale models were also used in some scenes). Meanwhile, the school's corridors were filmed in Gloucester Cathedral, and the courtyard in Durham Cathedral's cloisters. Oxford, the "city of spires," also played a major role in bringing Hogwarts to life. The scene where Harry visits the restricted section of the school library in *The Sorcerer's Stone* was filmed in Duke Humfrey's Library, the oldest reading room at the Bodleian (in case you're wondering, the flame in Harry's lantern was a CGI effect, with fire of any kind a strict no-no in the library). Hogwarts's Great Hall was based on the dining hall at Christ Church college, Oxford University, though the hall itself was recreated at Leavesden Studios, near London.

With this varied tapestry of shooting locations, Hogwarts castle expanded and transformed as each movie revealed new rooms, dungeons, and staircases. Luckily, any continuity glitches between movies can be easily explained away by the shapeshifting nature of the school's magical walls and staircases.

MUGGLE LIFE

Possibly the most famous cul-de-sac in England, Privet Drive, home of the Dursleys, was filmed on a close in Bracknell, Berkshire. From *The Chamber of Secrets* onward, a replica of the house was used instead.

In the fourth movie, Draco Malfoy turns into a ferret in Oxford's shady New College Courtyard.

Eilean na Moine
The tiny wooded island of Eilean na Moine, at the western end of Scotland's Loch Eilt, is the site of Albus Dumbledore's grave.

Glenfinnan Viaduct
A tardy Ron and Harry fly over this stone viaduct in *The Chamber of Secrets* after missing the *Hogwarts Express* from King's Cross.

③ ## Alnwick Castle
This 11th-century castle played the exterior of Hogwarts; the Outer Bailey was featured during broomstick lessons.

④ ## Goathland Station
This station on the heritage North Yorkshire Moors Railway is featured as Hogsmeade station, appearing prominently in the final scene of *The Sorcerer's Stone*.

⑤ ## Malham Cove
Harry and Hermione set up camp atop the cracked limestone of Malham Cove in *The Deathly Hallows: Part 1*.

Lavenham
This medieval village in Suffolk became Godric's Hollow, with the timbered De Vere House playing Harry's birthplace.

⑦ ## Virginia Water
These manicured gardens and lake stood in as areas of Hogwarts's grounds from *The Prisoner of Azkaban* onward.

⑧ ## Swinley Forest
Harry, Ron, and Hermione are captured by a group of Snatchers in this pine tree forest near Bracknell during *The Deathly Hallows: Part 1*.

⑨

Oxford
The city's famous Bodleian Library is seen in the first movie when Harry is recuperating in the Hogwarts infirmary.

⑩ ## Lacock Abbey
Snape's classroom was shot in The Sacristy here and the Mirror of Erised was stored in the Chapter House.

⑪ ## Gloucester Cathedral
The ornate stone cloisters of this cathedral doubled as Hogwarts's busy corridors.

⑫

Freshwater West
In *The Deathly Hallows: Part 1,* Dobby the house elf, Harry Potter's faithful companion, is buried on this dune-backed beach on the Pembrokeshire Coast. Many fans still make pilgrimages here to pay their respects to the free elf.

Inverness

① Eilean na Moine
② Glenfinnan Viaduct

Perth

SCOTLAND

Glasgow   Edinburgh

③ Alnwick Castle

Newcastle upon Tyne

Goathland Station ④

⑤ Malham Cove

Leeds

Liverpool

Manchester

ENGLAND

Birmingham

Gloucester Cathedral

WALES   Oxford   Lavenham ⑥
⑪   ⑨
Freshwater ⑫   Cardiff   *See London map, p78*
West   Bristol   ⑩   ⑧ ⑦

Swinley Forest, the setting for Harry, Ron, and Hermione's encounter with the Snatchers in the seventh movie.

London Zoo

Harry traps Dudley in a Burmese python enclosure in London Zoo's Reptile House. The area used in filming is now home to a (much more deadly) black mamba.

King's Cross Station

Filming of platform 9¾ took place between platforms 4 and 5. Look out for the gift shop beside platform 9 and a trolley disappearing into the wall.

3

Claremont Square

The Order of the Phoenix's hidden headquarters at Grimmauld Place can be seen (or maybe not) in Claremont Square.

4

Leadenhall Market

The Leaky Cauldron pub from the first movie was filmed in the spectacular Leadenhall Market (at the opticians at 2-3 Bull's Head Passage to be precise).

Great Scotland Yard

The office of the Ministry of Magic is located in the government heart of London. The phone box entrance on Great Scotland Yard was a prop.

5

7 Stoney St.

The Leaky Cauldron moves here in the third movie. Next door is Henry Pordes Books Ltd, which starred as the Third Hand Book Emporium in *The Chamber of Secrets*.

Map labels

- ① London Zoo
- *Regent's Park*
- CAMDEN
- ② King's Cross Station
- ③ Claremont Square
- FINSBURY
- **LONDON**
- BLOOMSBURY
- CLERKENWELL
- HOLBORN
- ⑧ Great Scotland Yard
- SOHO
- COVENT GARDEN
- CITY
- ④ Leadenhall Market
- ⑦ Australia House
- ⑥ Millennium Bridge
- *Thames*
- *River*
- SOUTH BANK
- ⑤ 7 Stoney St.
- SOUTHWARK
- *Hyde Park*
- *Green Park*
- KNIGHTSBRIDGE
- ⑨ Westminster Station
- WESTMINSTER
- LAMBETH
- PIMLICO

Westminster Station

Harry and Mr. Weasley venture through this tube station in *The Order of the Phoenix*. It's a rare example of filming being permitted in a working tube station.

Australia House

The striking marble entrance hall of Australia House was the ideal stand-in for Gringott's Wizarding Bank (it later appeared in *Wonder Woman [p42]*, too).

Millennium Bridge

This bridge is destroyed when Death Eaters attack London at the beginning of *The Half-Blood Prince*.

When the school term ends, Harry and his friends venture beyond the grounds of Hogwarts. London plays a central role in the wizarding world, with witches and wizards stocking up on all sorts of magical provisions in the bustling lanes of the UK capital. It's no surprise, then, that the Potter movies filmed extensively in the city. London's unique mishmash of architecture, along with its mazes of narrow streets, provided an entirely plausible location for a secret world hiding in plain sight. Part of the genius of Rowling's books is the way the magical sits side-by-side with the mundane—the saga's London-set sequences replicate a similar alchemy.

While the legendary Diagon Alley was built on a sound stage, the location for The Leaky Cauldron pub (the door to the wizarding world) was located in the historic Leadenhall Market. We also see London in *The Prisoner of Azkaban*, when Harry boards the lightning-quick Knight Bus. Stunt coordinator Greg Powell explained that the bus was driven at 30 mph (48 km/h) while cars slowly passed it at 8 mph (13 km/h). Even the people you see walking past on the street were trained to walk incredibly slowly to make the bus look even faster. The famous Gringotts bank, meanwhile, was realized in the marble halls of Australia House. As was the case with many of the real-life locations, a replica of the interior was built in the studio for later movies. This was undoubtedly a sensible idea; surely most landlords would take a dim view of ferocious Ukrainian Ironbelly dragons destroying a building.

The good news for the Potter faithful is that Gringotts—and numerous other sets—can be experienced firsthand at the Warner Bros. Studio Tour London: The Making of Harry Potter. The studio's detailed model of Hogwarts will make even the most cynical Muggle fall for the magic of the wizarding world. Offering the chance to see real props and witness the movies' spectacular visual effects (you'll soon believe a broomstick can fly), it's pure fan heaven.

The historic Leadenhall Market, site of The Leaky Cauldron pub

PADDINGTON

Following the adventures of Michael Bond's adorable Peruvian bear, this beloved movie series take viewers on a whirlwind tour of the capital's most scenic spots, from Primrose Hill to Portobello Road.

YEAR
2014, 2017

LOCATION
LONDON, ENGLAND

It took decades for Paddington Bear to make it to the big screen, but in 2014, fans finally got the movie they'd been waiting for. Directed by Paul King, *Paddington* takes the popular bear, created by British author Michael Bond in 1958, on a rip-roaring adventure around London. While delighting adults and children alike, the movie also acts as a love letter to the capital, showcasing the prettiest corners of the city through the wide eyes of the bear from "darkest Peru" (Costa Rica was used in the movie).

King's fantastical version of London—he described his vision for *Paddington* as "set in the world of *Amélie*"—meant that locations were selected both for their accuracy to the beloved books and for their aesthetic appeal on screen.

At the heart of it all is the charming Windsor Gardens, home of the Browns in both Bond's books and the movie. The equally charming Chalcot Crescent, a

The pastel-coloured Chalcot Crescent in Primrose Hill, home of the Browns

pastel-hued row of town houses in the Primrose Hill area of North London, was the ideal stand-in for this fairy-tale street. Beyond this, *Paddington*'s London almost works as a supercut of the city. Favorite corners, including Pall Mall, the Natural History Museum, and Portobello Road Market, all have their moment in the sun, creating an overtly positive and colorful version of London. And, of course, in the world of *Paddington,* they all feel a mere hop, skip, jump—or an umbrella-propelled skateboard ride—away from each other.

The sequel sees Paddington settling into his new home only to be framed and thrown in jail. These surprisingly heartwarming scenes, featuring a memorable turn by Brendan Gleeson as fellow inmate, prison chef Knuckles McGinty, were shot in Kilmainham Gaol in Dublin, with the Shepton Mallet Prison in Somerset used as the ominous exterior. While the ever-optimistic, marmalade-loving mammal tries to make the prison a better place, viewers are taken on another tour of London thanks to a pop-up book that doubles as a treasure map. It's an appropriately twee device that showcases famous locations such as St. Paul's Cathedral—and, fittingly, it's designed in the style of Peggy Fortnum, the original illustrator of the *Paddington* books.

6 Paddington Station
Commuters in Paddington station ignore the bear waiting patiently on platform 1.

1 Chalcot Crescent
This crescent doubles as Windsor Gardens, the home of Paddington and the Browns.

5 Alice's
The outside of Mr. Gruber Antiques was filmed at Alice's, a well-known antiques shop selling an assortment of vintage goods on London's Portobello Road.

2 St. Paul's Cathedral
In *Paddington 2*, the Browns follow Hugh Grant's Phoenix Buchanan to this landmark, one of the locations in the pop-up book.

4 Natural History Museum
The finale of the first movie is set in the Gothic halls of this museum, where the menacing Millicent Clyde is head taxidermist.

3 Reform Club
The bureaucratic Geographers' Guild was filmed inside the Reform Club, a private members' club on Pall Mall.

CAMDEN

Chalcot 1 Crescent

ST JOHN'S WOOD

Regent's Park

MAIDA VALE

NORTH KENSINGTON

MARYLEBONE

BLOOMSBURY

HOLBORN

Paddington 6 Station

LONDON

COVENT GARDEN

St. Paul's 2 Cathedral

CITY

BAYSWATER

SOHO

MAYFAIR

River Thames

5 Alice's

NOTTING HILL

Kensington Gardens

Hyde Park

Reform Club 3

3

KENSINGTON

KNIGHTSBRIDGE

VICTORIA

Natural History 4 Museum

EARL'S COURT

SOUTH KENSINGTON

PIMLICO

CHELSEA

GHOSTBUSTERS

No other '80s movie defined the Big Apple quite like *Ghostbusters*.
Shooting all around New York, director Ivan Reitman's movie reveled
in the city's energy, highlighting why so many of us "love this town."

YEAR
1984

LOCATION
NEW YORK, US

SNL stars, over-the-top special effects, and a New York City setting: *Ghostbusters* didn't exactly have the typical ingredients for a big-hitting blockbuster. But against the odds, this sci-fi adventure became one of the best New York-based movies of all time.

Following a quartet of paranormal pest controllers as they battle ghosts in New York, *Ghostbusters* masterfully mixes comedy, action, and horror. It was first conceived by Dan Aykroyd,

best-known for his work on *SNL* and his starring role in *The Blues Brothers* (1980). The writer/actor is fascinated with the supernatural and his original idea for the movie featured the crew on an intergalactic ghost-hunting mission, set in the future. When director Ivan Reitman came on board to help with the script, he suggested grounding the action in New York instead. The gritty city wasn't really a hive of production at the time—many movies were shot in

Hook & Ladder 8 Firehouse, the exterior of Ghostbusters HQ in New York City

②

Tavern on the Green
Louis's attempts to flee a terror dog see him unable to get into this exclusive Central Park restaurant.

①

Columbia University
After getting fired from this university, Ray, Venkman, and Egon discuss forming the Ghostbusters in the quad.

③

55 Central Park West
This was Louis and Dana Barrett's prestigious apartment block. The production team added eight floors, as well as the doglike gargoyles, through matte paintings to create the rooftop shrine.

④

Columbus Circle
The first sighting of the Stay-Puft Marshmallow Man was at the busy Columbus Circle. The buildings are now unrecognizable after decades of redevelopment.

⑤

Rockefeller Center
This New York landmark appears briefly in the energetic midmovie montage which illustrates the Ghostbusters' rise to fame.

⑥

New York Public Library
The opening scene in the Rose Main Reading Room was filmed in just a few hours, before the library fully opened at 10 a.m.

Los Angeles—and Reitman was warned that filming here could be tricky.

Part of what makes *Ghostbusters* such a perfect New York–based movie is the fact that so much of what you see on screen is genuinely New York. Reitman fully embraced the city, shooting scenes in various landmarks and making full use of the Gothic architecture and frenetic street energy. Filming in the Big Apple wasn't without its limitations, however. *Ghostbusters* opens at the New York Public Library, with the hulking lion statue in the foreground (New York's numerous statues are a running theme in the movie). The crew had to be in and out before the library opened to visitors, meaning the scene was largely shot in one take; when the librarian goes downstairs, she's in the Los Angeles Public Library instead. Guerrilla filming tactics were also used, most notably when the gang are seen running from the Rockefeller Center in the montage sequence. They were, in fact, running away from security guards as the crew couldn't get the proper filming permits.

Toward the movie's end, the group drive Ecto-1 (their limo-style car) uptown from their Tribeca neighborhood. To shoot this sequence, traffic in New York was shut down on 7th, 8th, and 9th avenues, resulting in such a build up of traffic that at one point almost two-thirds of the city was said to be in gridlock. While all of this was going on, sci-fi writer Isaac Asimov, who lived in the Upper West Side, came over to tell Aykroyd how furious he was that he couldn't get home. The author had no idea who he was talking to, nor that cinematic history was being made right before his eyes.

① Columbia University

UPPER WEST SIDE

Central Park

③ 55 Central Park West

② Tavern on the Green

④ Columbus Circle

HELL'S KITCHEN

⑤ Rockefeller Center

MIDTOWN WEST

⑥ New York Public Library

MIDTOWN EAST

MIDTOWN

MANHATTAN

CHELSEA

East River

GRAMERCY PARK

GREENWICH VILLAGE

NEW YORK CITY

SOHO

⑦ Hook & Ladder 8 Firehouse

LOWER EAST SIDE

LOWER MANHATTAN

Hudson River

⑦

Hook & Ladder 8 Firehouse
This fire station was Ghostbusters HQ in Tribeca, a neighborhood Egon called a "demilitarized zone." Interior scenes were shot in LA.

CENTRAL PARK

As do yellow taxis and towering skyscrapers, Central Park plays a key role in creating on-screen New York. Many scenes have unfolded in this lovely spot, including cherished family favorites.

In 1908, Central Park was used as the backdrop for a movie adaptation of *Romeo and Juliet*, and ever since, its magic has been an irresistible draw for filmmakers. Blanketing the middle of Manhattan, this famous swathe of green has been featured in movies and shows more than 350 times (and counting), from rom-coms like *Serendipity* (2001) to action movies such as *Die Hard with a Vengeance* (1995).

More than your fair share of family flicks have been filmed here, too. As well as appearing in *Ghostbusters (p82)*, the famed urban park was where a lost Kevin McCallister meets a warm-hearted pigeon lady in *Home Alone 2* (1992) and where Buddy the Elf saves Santa in Christmas favorite *Elf* (2003). Then there's *Enchanted* (2007), a modern-day fairy tale where the park puts its best foot forward. As Princess Giselle sings "That's How You Know," she flits between some of the park's most famous sights, among them Bethesda Fountain and Bow Bridge. And who can blame her? Central Park is pretty wonderful, after all.

BREAKFAST AT TIFFANY'S
(1961) ▶
The store may be the domain of main character Holly, but several Central Park spots, including Conservatory Water, are where Paul goes in his pensive moments.

WHEN HARRY MET SALLY
(1989)
This movie proves there's nothing like fall in New York. In one scene, Harry and Sally get to know each other better during a stroll under the park's orange leaves.

ELF (2003) ▶
Buddy the Elf tries to get Santa airborne again after he crash-lands in Central Park. They're chased by the evil park rangers, eventually escaping, thanks to a little bit of Christmas spirit.

GHOSTBUSTERS 2 (1989)
Jogging through Central Park is a quintessential New York experience, so it's no surprise that one of the many ghosts in this movie does exactly that.

INDIANA JONES

Indiana Jones is no ordinary archaeologist. On his quests to uncover ancient artifacts, this whip-wielding hero has ventured to some of the world's greatest wonders, taking an ever-captivated audience along for the ride.

YEAR
1981, 1984, 1989, 2008, 2023

LOCATION
WORLDWIDE

Al-Khazneh (The Treasury) in Petra, the setting for *The Last Crusade*'s final scene

The enduring legacy of Harrison Ford's intrepid Indiana Jones is undeniable. Everybody's favorite archaeologist turned action hero has been running from boulders, leaping off vehicles, and punching protagonists for decades—and he's still going strong. The adventures are undeniably thrilling, but they almost pale in comparison to the movies' striking locations. Jet-setting around countries like Tunisia, Sri Lanka, and Spain, the *Indiana Jones* franchise is nearly as well-traveled as *James Bond (p186)*.

The movie that started it all, *Raiders of the Lost Ark*, was the brainchild of *Star Wars (p166)* creator George Lucas. Inspired by the action protagonists of his favorite 1930s- and '40s-era films, Lucas wanted to make a B-movie focused on the high-octane adventures of an archaeologist named Indiana Smith (the second name didn't stick). He didn't want to direct, however; that role would go to fellow movie fanatic Steven Spielberg.

Raiders of the Lost Ark began filming in June 1980, with a $20 million budget and a tight 73-day shooting schedule in Tunisia. This north African country, which Lucas was familiar with after shooting *Star Wars* there, was chosen as

Harrison Ford (Indiana Jones) filming
Raiders of the Lost Ark in Tunisia

a substitute for Egypt. While Tunisia's vast deserts were a perfect stand-in, just as in *Star Wars,* Lucas faced numerous issues while filming here. Temperatures rose to a toasty 129°F (54°C), giving the producer terrible sunburn; dysentery also took out around 150 crew members, including Harrison Ford. The actor was set to film an epic sword and whip battle (which would normally take days to shoot) but was

DID YOU KNOW?

INDY'S HOME
The hero's home in *The Last Crusade* now operates as a B&B in Antonito, Colorado.

CLUB OBI WAN
At the beginning of *The Temple of Doom,* Indy enters a club named after the Jedi master from *Star Wars (p166),* in a tribute to George Lucas.

9,000
An estimated 9,000 snakes and legless lizards were in the Well of Souls in *Raiders of the Lost Ark.* Luckily, Harrison Ford isn't scared of snakes like Indy is.

feeling so ill he suggested Indy just shoot the guy. Happily, the director agreed, and the comical scene is now one of the most lauded in the franchise.

For the movie's sequel, *Indiana Jones and the Temple of Doom*, Lucas swapped the deserts of Tunisia for the jungles of Sri Lanka. A key scene sees Indy meet his foes on a rope bridge, before swiftly sending them into the crocodile-infested water below; this temporary bridge was built over Sri Lanka's stunning Mahaweli River. While the weather stayed on side this time around, *The Temple of Doom*'s shoot wasn't all smooth sailing. Ford suffered a severe spinal injury on set and had to fly back to the US; his stuntman, Vic Armstrong, subbed in as Indy for some scenes.

Indiana Jones and the Last Crusade was indeed a crusade, with scenes shot at various locations around Europe and the Middle East. For the sinister majesty

ACCESS DENIED
The Indian government thought *The Temple of Doom*'s depiction of its people as brutal antagonists and voodoo practitioners was offensive. They requested script changes, but couldn't come to an agreement with the production team, so filming moved to Sri Lanka instead.

of Castle Brunwald, where Indy's father is held captive, the crew used exterior shots of Germany's Bürresheim Castle. To make it unique, they flipped the castle's image on-screen and expanded its exterior with matte painting. After an exciting adventure with his father, Indy ends his quest for the Holy Grail at Al-Khazneh (The Treasury), an incredible sandstone structure in the ancient

Sri Lanka's Mahaweli River, the location of the rope bridge in *The Temple of Doom*

city of Petra, in Jordan. Built by the Nabataeans in the middle of the desert, this rock-carved city gained UNESCO World Heritage status in 1985 and found cinematic fame after the finale was shot here. Numerous movies, including *The Mummy Returns* (2001) and *Transformers: Revenge of the Fallen* (2009), have since utilized its ancient desert scenery.

Taking full advantage of Indy's globe-trotting tendencies, the third episode of *Indiana Jones* truly cemented Indy as a legendary action hero. His adventures aren't over yet, however: 2023's *Indiana Jones and the Dial of Destiny* sees the protagonist back in his saddle, whip in hand and ready for one more movie before his retirement.

(1)

Bürresheim Castle
Indy and his father reunite at this stunning castle in Germany during *The Last Crusade*.

(2)

Venice
In the third movie, Indy's father's diary leads the hero to the Chiesa di San Barnaba.

(3) **Al-Khazneh, Petra**
Exterior shots in *The Last Crusade*'s climax were filmed at Jordan's Treasury building in Petra.

(4)

Tozeur
The dig site in *Raiders of the Lost Ark* was located near the Tunisian city of Tozeur.

Not far from the city is the rocky Jebel Sidi Bouhlel (Maguer Gorge), where the Nazis transport the Ark before opening it. The area is also known as the "Star Wars Canyon" after featuring prominently in *Star Wars: A New Hope*.

(5)

Kairouan
This Tunisian city doubled as the Old Medina of Cairo in *Raiders of the Lost Ark*. Indy famously shoots the swordsman in Kairouan's Place J'raba.

(6)

Almería
The third movie sees Indy's father using an umbrella to crash an attacking aircraft on the Playa de Mónsul.

(7) **Tabernas**
Indy battles to rescue his father from a German tank in this Spanish desert.

GERMANY
BELGIUM
1 Bürresheim Castle
FRANCE
SWITZ.
CZECH REPUBLIC
SLOVAKIA
AUSTRIA
HUNGARY
SLOVENIA
Venice 2
BOSNIA-HERZ.
SERBIA
ROMANIA
ITALY
BULGARIA
N. MAC
SPAIN
Tabernas 7
6 Almería
Kairouan 5
TURKEY
Tozeur 4
Mediterranean Sea
SYRIA
MOROCCO
ALGERIA
TUNISIA
JORDAN
EGYPT
Al-Khazneh, Petra 3
LIBYA

BACK TO THE FUTURE

Great Scott! Just as the time-traveling adventures of Doc and Marty McFly remained in Hill Valley, *Back to the Future's* production strayed little farther than Los Angeles.

YEAR
1985, 1989, 1990

LOCATION
CALIFORNIA, US

Appropriately for a movie that's all about things turning out differently, there's an alternate reality in which Michael J. Fox doesn't play *Back to the Future's* Marty McFly. For the first six weeks of filming, Eric Stoltz donned McFly's red puffer jacket until director Robert Zemeckis, unhappy with Stoltz's overly serious performance, fired him. Fox nabbed the role and ended up working 16-hour days, shooting his sitcom *Family Ties* and the movie simultaneously.

It must have made things easier for Fox that the bulk of filming took place at the Courthouse Square set in Universal Studios, LA. Appearing in multiple movies over the years (including 1962's *To Kill a Mockingbird*), this recreation of a typical American square became Hill Valley's downtown area. Over the course of the trilogy, it was redressed to reflect three different time periods: 1985, 1955, and the futuristic 2015. Here, you'll find

Back to the Future's much-featured Clocktower, which is hit by lightning in the first movie. The clock is still there (no longer frozen in time), but the building's facade has changed slightly since the wily Doc dangled from it.

While production relied heavily on the set, the team did venture into LA when more locations were needed, so fans don't need to join the studio tour to go back to the ... past.

Hill Valley's Clocktower, at Universal Studios

① **Port Hueneme**
The Delorean is destroyed on the railroad tracks at South Ventura Road and Shoreview Drive in Port Hueneme in the third film.

② **Universal Studios Backlot**
Occasionally included on the studio tour, Courthouse Square was downtown Hill Valley in the first two *Back to the Future* movies.

③

Hollywood United Methodist Church
Marty McFly takes to the stage during the first movie's "Enchantment Under the Sea" dance, shot at this church.

④ **Mt. Hollywood Tunnel**
This tunnel in Griffith Park is where Biff tries to crush Marty and his hoverboard in the second movie.

⑤

Gamble House
Back in 1955, Doc's family house was the Gamble House, an Arts and Crafts architectural gem.

⑥

Puente Hills Mall
Doc introduces his time machine to Marty in the parking lot of this local mall.

GROUNDHOG DAY

The city of Woodstock found fame in director Harold Ramis's time-loop comedy, which sees a curmudgeonly Bill Murray forced to relive the same day over and over and...

YEAR
1993

LOCATION
ILLINOIS, US

In this metaphysical masterpiece, the city of Woodstock, Illinois, stands in for Punxsutawney, Pennsylvania—the town where the real Groundhog Festival takes place every year. It begs the question: why didn't Harold Ramis shoot the movie in Punxsutawney?

In reality, the festival takes place in a park on the outskirts of Punxsutawney, but Ramis wanted his version of the town and event to have an altogether more close-knit feel, with a gathering point at its heart. The director scouted over 60 locations, but when he rolled into Woodstock—with its picture-perfect town square, white picket fences, and small-town streets—he knew that his search was over. Filming took place all around the city, with the main square and its bandstand appearing regularly; on the north side of the square is a plaque showing where the beleaguered Phil steps, repeatedly, into an icy puddle. A short walk from here, you'll find the cute Cherry Tree Inn B&B *(p92)*, where Phil furiously wakes every morning.

The city of Woodstock has changed little since it became Phil's purgatory, and today, you can almost follow in his exact footsteps. Word of warning if you do, though: watch that first step.

ROOM SERVICE

What better way to experience a movie than to stay where it was shot? The list of gorgeous hotels and homes featured on screen is endless, and luckily, many of them are open for visitors.

GROUNDHOG DAY (1993)
Cherry Tree Inn B&B, Illinois, US

The quaint B&B where Phil of *Groundhog Day (p91)* wakes every morning with increasing frustration is, in fact, a charming Midwestern inn. Book a stay here and head out on the self-guided movie tour (just avoid playing *that* Sonny and Cher tune while you're there).

DIRTY DANCING (1987)
Mountain Lake Lodge, Virginia, US

Dirty Dancing's leafy summer retreat, Kellerman's, was set in the real-life Mountain Lake Lodge. Most of the movie was shot at this rustic hotel in Virginia, where visitors can still stay today to enjoy themed weekends and tours of the filming locations.

THE SHINING (1980)
Timberline Lodge, Oregon, US

While the majority of *The Shining* *(p114)* was filmed at Elstree Studios in England, the exterior of the Overlook Hotel was shot at the wooden Timberline Lodge. This snowbound ski lodge, tucked away in Oregon's remote and mountainous surrounds, is the perfect setting for the movie's psychological horror. Visit on Halloween for an extra spooky stay.

EX MACHINA (2014)
Juvet Landscape Hotel, Alstad, Norway

The main filming location in Alex Garland's eerie sci-fi *Ex Machina*, the home of reclusive CEO Nathan is stylish and suitably secluded. To create the ideal setting, scenes were filmed across two buildings: a hotel in Norway and a private home. You can stay at the former, the luxurious Juvet Landscape Hotel, in rooms that celebrate the beauty of the surrounding nature. The Roy family also stays in this same hotel in *Succession* (2018–2023), when the team take a trip to Norway.

CRAZY RICH ASIANS (2018)
Marina Bay Sands, Singapore

An icon itself, the Marina Bay Sands hotel was the setting for Rachel and Nick's farewell party in this swish rom-com drama. You'll have to fork out a fortune to stay here, but the swoon-worthy infinity pool and 360-degree views of Singapore are hard to find anywhere else.

1 Cherry Tree Inn, where Phil's day would start the same way again and again

2 The *Dirty Dancing* legacy at Mountain Lake Lodge

3 Oregon's remote Timberline Lodge

4 One of the rooms at the Juvet Landscape Hotel

5 It's all glitz and glamour at Marina Bay Sands, the ideal party setting for *Crazy Rich Asians*

1

2

Kellerman's
Mountain House
MOUNTAIN LAKE WELCOMES YOU

3

4

5

JURASSIC PARK

Hawaii's rainforest-cloaked island of Kaua'i was the perfect setting for this Spielberg smash hit. Visit today and it's not hard to imagine a *Tyrannosaurus rex* lurking amid the dense foliage.

YEAR
**1993, 1997, 2001,
2015, 2018, 2022**

LOCATION
HAWAII, US

When Steven Spielberg does spectacle, he goes big—just ask the generations of fans who have scenes from *Jurassic Park* seared into their memory. Who can forget that first thrilling glimpse of a brachiosaurus eating leaves from a tree or the arrival of the T. rex with those ominous ripples? The dinosaurs may get all the glory, but credit is also due to the lush foliage of Hawaii. After all, the park at the center of the story would never have felt so lifelike without a backdrop that was so perfectly prehistoric.

While Michael Crichton's source novel was set in Costa Rica, concerns about road infrastructure and accessibility led the director to shoot most of the movie on the Hawaiian island of Kaua'i. He was already familiar with the location, having filmed the first scene of *Raiders of the Lost Ark (p87)* here—in fact, Spielberg originally approached Harrison Ford for Sam Neill's role of Dr. Alan Grant. But this time around there was something unexpected to contend with: where there are tropical paradises, there are also tropical storms. A few weeks in,

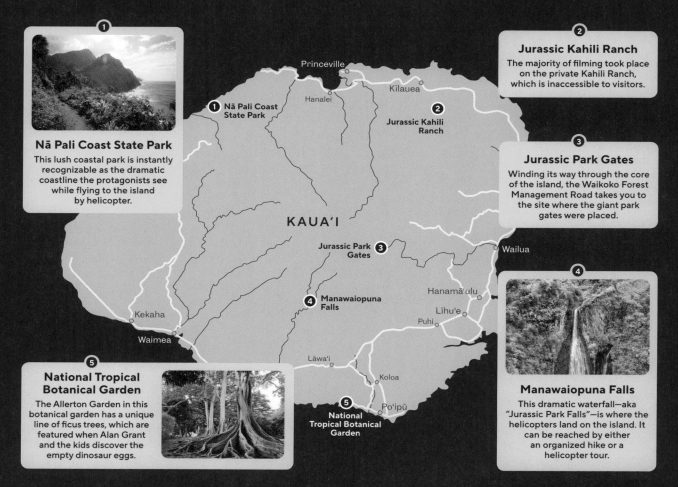

Nā Pali Coast State Park
This lush coastal park is instantly recognizable as the dramatic coastline the protagonists see while flying to the island by helicopter.

Jurassic Kahili Ranch
The majority of filming took place on the private Kahili Ranch, which is inaccessible to visitors.

Jurassic Park Gates
Winding its way through the core of the island, the Waikoko Forest Management Road takes you to the site where the giant park gates were placed.

Manawaiopuna Falls
This dramatic waterfall—aka "Jurassic Park Falls"—is where the helicopters land on the island. It can be reached by either an organized hike or a helicopter tour.

National Tropical Botanical Garden
The Allerton Garden in this botanical garden has a unique line of ficus trees, which are featured when Alan Grant and the kids discover the empty dinosaur eggs.

FILMING IN THE ALOHA STATE

Hawaii's greenery has provided a backdrop for more than just dinosaurs, eaturing in everything from rom-coms to drama series.

50 FIRST DATES
(2004)

Most of this romance was shot on the Windward Coast of O'ahu. The movie's diner (which was a set) was based on the Hukilau Cafe in Laie.

- - - - - - - - - - - - - - - - -

THE WHITE LOTUS
(2021–)

This universally acclaimed show always features the most beautiful locations; season 1 took place at the Four Seasons Resort Maui.

- - - - - - - - - - - - - - - - -

LOST
(2004–2010)

This survival series was largely shot on the island of O'ahu; the pilot took place at Mokulē'ia Beach.

Jurassic Park's shoot was impacted by Hurricane Iniki, one of the costliest and most powerful hurricanes to hit Hawaii. Luckily no one from the movie's cast or production crew was harmed in the storm—perhaps most miraculously, Richard Attenborough (who played park owner John Hammond) managed to sleep right through it while everyone else hunkered in the hotel basement. The set was not so fortunate, however. The structures that Spielberg's team had so meticulously built, including the towers that contained the park's power controls, were (much like the poor cow that is lowered into the velociraptor pen) torn to pieces.

With only one day left to shoot, scenes were dropped and production moved to the island of O'ahu. Here, Spielberg shot the scene where Grant and the children cower behind a felled tree to shield from the terrifying dinosaur stampede. The director also turned the storm to his advantage, including shots of Hurricane Iniki in the finished cut; around the 54-minute mark you can see glimpses of the residual storm, with huge waves crashing along the shore. After taking these final shots, Spielberg then dashed off to Poland to film *Schindler's List*, reluctantly approving the T. rex footage via "a very crude satellite feed."

Kaua'i would soon return to its idyllic appearance and the *Jurassic Park* series—including *Jurassic Park III* (2001) and *Jurassic World* (2015)—would continue to shoot on the Hawaiian islands, among other places. Plenty of locations from the franchise can still be seen on Kaua'i and O'ahu—a miniature tourist industry has even sprung up, giving enthusiasts tours of some of the most memorable places. Those who venture here can expect to find the mountains, coastlines, and waterfalls

of Hawaii just as captivating and awe-inspiringly beautiful as they are on-screen. Here, even without Spielberg's impressive sets (or deadly dinosaurs), the junglelike rainforest feels like its own prehistoric paradise—so much so that the slightest ripple of a puddle is still likely to send a shiver down your spine.

Kualoa Ranch on O'ahu, star of both *Jurassic Park* and *Jurassic World*

A brachiosaurus, as seen in the first movie

PIRATES OF THE CARIBBEAN

As the name dictated, this swashbuckling series shot across the idyllic islands of the Caribbean, but remote beaches, tropical storms, and a lack of infrastructure meant filming wasn't always smooth sailing.

YEAR
2003, 2006, 2007, 2011, 2017

LOCATION
THE CARIBBEAN

There were doubts about *Pirates of the Caribbean* from the very start. Not only did the movie raise eyebrows with its source material (a theme park ride), it also marked the return of the pirate-movie genre, which (most presumed) had died a death with box office flop *Cutthroat Island* (1995). Five installments later, however, *Pirates of the Caribbean* has become one of Disney's most successful franchises. It even earned Johnny Depp an Oscar nomination for his role as Captain Jack Sparrow, a performance he based on Rolling Stones's guitarist Keith Richards.

While some of the movies' sets were created in California (the treasure cave in the first movie took nearly five months to build from scratch), much of the movie was shot around various countries in the Caribbean. These beautiful locations played a huge part in giving the series its distinctive look and set the scene for Sparrow's various escapades. Kicking off the series, *The Curse of the Black Pearl* (2003) primarily shot at the

Idyllic Wallilabou Bay, the perfect setting for Port Royal

resort of Wallilabou Anchorage, on St. Vincent's Wallilabou Bay. (Disney's scouts mainly chose it because it was one of the few resorts that wasn't teeming with people.) The hotel's shops and restaurant were transformed into the pirate city of Port Royal, with the studio adding two new piers. Hurricanes destroyed the main pier in 2004, but remarkably, the rest of the set remained intact and was used again for the 2006 sequel, *Dead Man's Chest*. It still stands today and even hosts a themed museum.

Dominica's tropical terrain was the perfect backdrop for Sparrow's second movie outing, but there was one snag: the island had limited transportation infrastructure, especially for 500 staff and tons of equipment. The production crew had to build roads to reach the mountains and beaches they wanted to shoot at. Many of the team also stayed on different islands, due to the lack of hotels, and had to sail to work every day, sometimes in torrential rain.

After five swashbuckling episodes, the *Pirates of the Caribbean* ended in 2017 and everybody's favorite pirate hung up his hat. You can still follow in his footsteps however, whether you're riding Disney's popular theme park ride or swaggering along the beaches of the Caribbean.

DISNEY RIDES THAT BECAME MOVIES

TOWER OF TERROR
(1997)

Partly shot at the attraction itself (in Walt Disney World Resort Orlando), this movie follows a journalist and his niece as they investigate disappearances in a haunted hotel. A new adaptation is in development, produced by Scarlett Johansson, who will also star in the movie.

THE HAUNTED MANSION
(2003)

This supernatural comedy stars Eddie Murphy and is based on the creepy ride that opened in Disney's Orlando resort in 1969. It was filmed on the massive Sable Ranch set in Santa Clarita, California, and in New Orleans.

JUNGLE CRUISE
(2021)

Based on the popular riverboat ride, and supposedly set on the Amazon, the Dwayne Johnson–starring movie was filmed mostly on the Hawaiian island of Kaua'i. The production team built a full 1916-style marketplace, tavern, and dock.

①

Isla Palominitos

On Stranger Tides (2011) sees Jack Sparrow leave Angelica on this tiny coral reef cay off Puerto Rico.

②

Dominica

The memorable water wheel fight in *Dead Man's Chest* (2006) was filmed near the village of Vieille Case on the north coast of Dominica.

While trapped in a cage made of bones, Will Turner and his cohorts tumble down hills and crash into trees before ending up in Dominica's Titou Gorge in *Dead Man's Chest*.

④

Petit Tabac

Jack Sparrow and Elizabeth Swan are abandoned on this island by Captain Barbossa; they manage to escape by burning some rum.

Isla Palominitos

① PUERTO RICO

VIRGIN ISLANDS

ANTIGUA

ST. KITTS and NEVIS

GUADELOUPE

Dominica **②**

MARTINIQUE

Caribbean Sea

SAINT LUCIA

ST. VINCENT and THE GRENADINES

③ Wallilabou Bay

④ Petit Tabac

GRENADA

TRINIDAD and TOBAGO

③

Wallilabou Bay

The Wallilabou Anchorage resort on this bay became Port Royal, the movie's infamous pirate city.

4

THE HORROR OF IT ALL

Our nightmares come in countless guises: a clown's deadpan laughter, the distant howl of a hungry werewolf, the circling fin of a great white shark. Whatever the phobia, the horror genre invites us to face it from the relative comfort of our sofas or theater seats. We can revel in dread without consequence—with our hands placed firmly over our eyes when it gets too much.

The locations in which these horrors play out are as varied as our fears themselves. No longer are tales of terror confined to the haunted house, as peril can be conjured anywhere: a sinister hotel isolated in the snowy mountains, a small town with a big secret, or the darkest depths of the ocean. A good location heightens the creeping anxiety and makes those jump scares all the more visceral. And knowing that no location is off limits is enough to keep the fear alive long after the credits have rolled.

THE WICKER MAN

Shot on location across Scotland's southwest coast, *The Wicker Man* added another legend to the wild countryside where selkies and faeries were already said to frolic.

YEAR
1973

LOCATION
SCOTLAND

Set on the fictional island of Summerisle, *The Wicker Man* (based on David Pinner's 1967 novel *Ritual*) sees an isolated community swept up in pagan worship. Director Robin Hardy needed a similarly isolated location to step in for this unreal world, and Scotland—then still known for its pockets of puritan society—fit the bill.

While *The Wicker Man*'s story takes place in the spring, the movie was actually shot during the cold months of October and November. Falling leaves and bare branches would've given the game away, so the team had to alter the natural surroundings at every new location: truckloads of fake apple blossom trees were brought in, while artificial leaves and spring flowers were laboriously glued to the wintry trees. This wasn't a viable option for the film's opening scenes, however, and so production swapped in aerial shots filmed in South Africa instead.

The chilly weather was also an issue. For the movie's climax—when Sergeant Howie, who comes to the island in search of a missing girl, finally meets the titular Wicker Man—Edward Woodward was dressed in just a simple shift, with his feet bare. Sure, his character had bigger worries, but the actor was very uncomfortable. Between takes, he'd scurry straight to actress Ingrid Pitt, who played the local librarian, and warm his feet under her wool skirt.

For the sinister finale, the filmmakers actually built two Wicker Men: a large one, which was used for the scenes where Woodward had to be inside it, and a smaller one for long shots. The original legs of the full-size one were

Culzean Castle, where exterior shots of Lord Summerisle's grand home were taken

① Culzean Castle

The scenic Culzean Castle, which dates from the 18th century, was the opulent residence of Lord Summerisle.

② Creetown

Tucked away in the tranquil seaside town of Creetown is the 19th-century Ellangowan Hotel. The internal shots of the island's Green Man pub were filmed here.

Focusing on the history of the town, Creetown Heritage Museum may not be featured in the movie, but it does have a display dedicated to it, complete with a small Wicker Man.

⑥ Kirkcudbright

The church Howie attends in the opening scene of the movie is located in this quaint town, as is May Morrison's Post Office, which was shot at 84 High Street.

Firth of Clyde

① Culzean Castle

○ Dalmellington

○ Girvan

SCOTLAND

Dumfries ○

Gretna ○

Newton Stewart ○

Castle Douglas ○

Anwoth Old Kirk

Stranraer ○

Creetown ②

⑤

Kirkcudbright

⑥

Luce Bay

Solway Firth

St. Ninians Cave ③ ④ Burrow Head

ENGLAND

③ St. Ninian's Cave

The May Day parade that Howie infiltrates ends at this cave. It's here that he finally sees Rowan, the missing girl, and attempts to rescue her.

④ Burrow Head

Both the small and large Wicker Man statues stood on the cliffs of Burrow Head, overlooking the chilly Irish sea. Neither statue remains and the area is now a caravan park.

⑤ Anwoth Old Kirk

Howie explores the remains of this church graveyard, which has changed little since the 1970s. The building where Summerisle school was set is just opposite.

still in place on the clifftop at Burrow Head in 2006, when someone sawed them off. Now, all that's left, unfortunately, is a concrete base.

On its release in 1973, *The Wicker Man* received little help from the studio, who put it out as a supporting feature to another British horror: *Don't Look Now (p124)*. The move infuriated actor Christopher Lee (who had played Lord Summerisle for no fee to ensure the movie happened) and he championed the film at every opportunity. As Sergeant Howie found out, you don't mess with Lord Summerisle—*The Wicker Man* has gone down in movie

STRANGER THINGS

The fictional town of Hawkins, Indiana (in reality, the charming Jackson, Georgia) is the epicenter of *Stranger Things*' mysterious world, a place continually plagued by the Upside Down.

Hawkins Middle School, the repurposed Patrick Henry Adult Education

YEAR
2016–

LOCATION
GEORGIA, US

It's hard to imagine today's television landscape without *Stranger Things*. This smash-hit Netflix show—which follows a group of friends as they battle against evil forces from an alternative dimension (the Upside Down)—turned its roster of up-and-coming actors into international superstars, and put the loud fashion and music of the 1980s back on the radar. While the show's cast of beloved characters and twisted, supernatural storylines drew in scores of fans, its setting, the fictional town of Hawkins, Indiana, was just as important to *Stranger Things*' world-wide success.

Butts County Courthouse, or Hawkins Library, where Hopper conducts research in season 1

THE MONTAUK PROJECT

At one point in its development, *Stranger Things* was called Montauk, in reference to the Montauk Project. This major government conspiracy theory—about mind control experiments on children in Montauk—originated in the 1980s and was the basis for *Stranger Things*' storyline.

Stranger Things' creators Matt and Ross Duffer initially wanted to shoot in Long Island, where the coastal village of Montauk (the setting for the original storyline) is located, but their plans soon changed. Instead, the brothers headed to the Atlanta area, which was reminiscent of their southern childhood homes. Here, they found Jackson, a tiny town less than 50 miles (80 km) from the city, with deep surrounding forests and an "Anytown, USA" feel to it; its blank urban canvas was the last place you'd expect evil and secret experiments to occur. Location chosen, production designer Chris Trujillo and his team set about sending Jackson back in time to the 1980s. They found vintage items at estate sales and scored Hopper's trailer home for just $1.

Jackson's 2nd Street, with its quaint storefronts and tree-lined sidewalks, became downtown Hawkins. Several characters' workplaces can be found here, including Joyce Byers's Melvald's General Store and "superhero" Bob Newby's Radio Shack. In reality, the buildings are a Papa John's pizzeria and a small juice bar, respectively, set-dressed for the show.

While the first two seasons of *Stranger Things* centered around Hawkins, the later seasons ventured outside of town. Season 3 focused on the ultimate 1980s teen hangout of the mall. Production scouted for a mostly "dead mall" to build a set worthy of a showdown between Eleven (who has psychokinetic abilities) and the Mind Flayer (an evil monster from the Upside Down). The dwindling Gwinnett Place, an hour or so north of Jackson, was perfect. Over ten weeks, the crew transformed the space into the dazzling Starcourt Mall, painting old structures and redressing vacant spaces with neon lighting. The team also created 40 new businesses in the mall, including Star Cinemas. These stores were even fully stocked just in case the need should arrive—and it did. In season 3, episode 2, friends Eleven and Max go on a joy-filled shopping spree.

As the show continued on for more record-breaking seasons, the locations expanded to other US states. The city of Albuquerque, New Mexico, became Lenora Hills, California, the desert town where Eleven and the Byers move to start a new life in season 4. However, the heart of each season still revolves around Hawkins. While the final season of *Stranger Things* is set to end the fight against the Upside Down, Jackson will always be there if you're looking to take a trip down the rabbit hole (or rather, the sludgy portal hidden in a tree).

The tree-lined Stone Mountain Railroad, a feature of season 1

MARIETTA
SANDY SPRINGS
NORCROSS
9 Gwinnett Place Mall
PLEASANT HILL
DALLAS
SMYRNA
VININGS
BROOKHAVEN
TUCKER
MOUNTAIN PARK
POWDER SPRINGS
MABLETON
3 Tiffany's Kitchen
Stone Mountain Cemetery
8
10 Stone Mountain Railroad
Family Video **2**
Arcade **1**
DOUGLASVILLE
Bellwood **5** Quarry
7 Emory Briarcliff Campus
ATLANTA
DECATUR
REDAN
BEN HILL
EAST POINT
6 South Bend Pool
STONECREST
CONYERS
Brimborn Steelworks **4**
FOREST PARK
UNION CITY
RIVERDALE
STOCKBRIDGE
12 Patrick Henry Adult Education
PALMETTO
JONESBORO
Piggly Wiggly **11**
FAYETTEVILLE
MCDONOUGH
13 Jackson

① Arcade
A disused laundromat at 6500 Church Street, in Douglasville, became the arcade in season 2.

② Family Video
Robin and Steve work in this video store, just next door to the arcade, in season 4.

③ Tiffany's Kitchen
Eleven sneaks into Benny's Burgers in season 1. You can have a burger in the same location, Tiffany's Kitchen, today.

④ Brimborn Steelworks
In season 3, Max's brother Billy is attacked by the Mind Flayer here.

⑤

Bellwood Quarry
Eleven showcases her powers at this quarry in season 1.

⑥

South Bend Pool
Billy worked at the Hawkins Community Swimming Pool in season 3, which was filmed at the South Bend Pool.

⑦

Emory Briarcliff Campus
This hulking building is the Hawkins National Laboratory, where Eleven opens the gate to the Upside Down. The building is due to be demolished in the near future.

⑧ Stone Mountain Cemetery
Max is entranced by Vecna while visiting Billy's grave here in season 4.

⑨

Gwinnett Place Mall
The vacant Gwinnett Place Mall was restyled as the Starcourt Mall.

⑩ Stone Mountain Railroad
In a homage to Stephen King's *Stand By Me*, the kids walk along this railroad beside Hawkins Lab in season 1.

⑪ Piggly Wiggly
This store in Palmetto was the site of Eleven's Eggos heist in season 1. Signs and photos show where the scene took place.

⑫ Patrick Henry Adult Education
This now-closed school became both Hawkins high and middle schools; the school is set to be demolished.

⑬ Jackson
This town played Hawkins, Indiana. Joyce's workplace, Melvald's General Store, is at 4 2nd Street while Hawkins' Radio Shack is at 11 2nd Street.

Lübeck's Salzspeicher, home to Nosferatu

NOSFERATU

A classic of German Expressionist cinema, this silent horror film relies on the physical performance of Max Shreck for its thrills, as well as a number of spectacular Gothic filming locations.

YEAR
1922

LOCATION
GERMANY; SLOVAKIA

Director F. W. Murnau's *Nosferatu* has proved almost as difficult to kill as its villain. Every copy of the unauthorized film was supposed to have been destroyed after the widow of Bram Stoker (the author of *Dracula*) won her plagiarism case against the production company. While she managed to get rid of most of the prints, she didn't get them all—several incomplete prints survived and were later restored.

Fittingly, many of the film's notable locations still stand to this day, despite being hundreds of years old. Portraying Count Orlok's (the eponymous vampire Nosferatu) Gothic home—with its dark

windows and shadowy staircases—was Lübeck's Salzspeicher. Dating to 1579, this distinctive brick building was once a salt warehouse. It's since been converted into a department store, so you may have to work your way past clothing racks to see the famous window where the Count spies on Hutter's wife, Ellen.

Nosferatu's castle in Transylvania was actually Orava Castle in Slovakia. Built in the 13th century, it sits high above the Orava River on a rock formation. It was originally a fort, then a residence and a museum. Orlok might have been the first vampire to succumb to sunlight, but some things, it seems, last forever.

NIGHT OF THE LIVING DEAD

George A. Romero needed only a Pennsylvanian farmhouse and a quiet cemetery to completely reimagine the zombie horror genre for his modern paranoia tale.

YEAR
1968

LOCATION
PENNSYLVANIA, US

As cult as they come, *Night of the Living Dead* tells the tale of undead "ghouls" (the director George A. Romero never explicitly called them zombies) running riot in rural America. Budgets for the movie were low and film experience was lacking, but that didn't stop Romero and his friends, writer John Russo and producer Russell Streiner, from creating a classic.

Bringing horror to the countryside, *Night of the Living Dead* filmed around Pennsylvania's Evans City, not far from the friends' workplace in Pittsburgh. The team liked the middle-of-nowhere feel to the area—and they didn't have the money to create the monstrous sets of the Hammer Horror movies that came before them anyway. Unassuming Evans City, with its sweeping fields and old farmhouses, would have to do.

The iconic opening scene sees the siblings Barbra and Johnny attacked by a disheveled townsman in the isolated Evans City Cemetery. Chosen for its secrecy at the time, away from curious onlookers or the police, the graveyard has become the movie's most famed location (it's also the only main location still standing). The headstone Barbra clutches in the opening scene and the cemetery's chapel are now popular spots for film pilgrims. The movie's other location, the Ash Stop Road farmhouse (where Barbra and her acquaintances try, unsuccessfully, to find shelter) was chosen by Romero because it was due to be demolished soon after filming. This gave the director and his cast of local amateurs license to do as they pleased: cue a mess of guts (ham from the local butcher), blood (chocolate syrup), and broken doors. The cast didn't take it too far, however—some of the crew were actually staying in the farmhouse while they were filming.

Romero's second zombie feature *Dawn of the Dead* (1978) saw the action move to Monroeville Mall, Pennsylvania. Clearly, neither countryside nor cities are safe from the deadly "ghouls."

OAKLEY COURT

With its grimacing gargoyles and soaring turret, this Gothic mansion could have jumped straight out of a horror movie. And it has—on more than one occasion.

Despite its tranquil setting in England's Berkshire countryside, Oakley Court gives off sinister vibes. While some might attribute this to ghosts (the house is reputedly haunted), its eeriness is more to do with its ties to Hammer Horror. Set up in 1934, this movie studio became famous for its extravagant horror flicks, with many of them shot at the Victorian mansion. Two of the most famous are the gory *The Curse of Frankenstein* (1957) and the lavishly produced, blood thirsty *Dracula* (1958). Both movies were big box office hits, capturing the attention of audiences and cementing Hammer as the head honchos of horror.

While Oakley Court has lost some of its fright factor, transforming from the home of Hammer to a luxury hotel, a glimpse of its Gothic exterior on a dark and shadowy night is enough to make anyone jump.

THE BRIDES OF DRACULA (1960) ▶
In the sequel to *Horror of Dracula*, Van Helsing (played by Peter Cushing) watches the vampire escape by coach from outside of the mansion.

THE CURSE OF FRANKENSTEIN (1957)
Hammer's first foray into Gothic horrors, this movie sees Baron and Dr. Krempe return to Oakley Court after killing the creature and burying it in the woods.

THE ROCKY HORROR
PICTURE SHOW (1975) ▶
In this cult movie, Oakley Court
was the setting for Dr. Frank N
Furter's eccentric castle (also
known as the Frankenstein Place),
with many scenes shot here.

MUMSY, NANNY, SONNY,
AND GIRLY (1970)
Written with Oakley Court in
mind, thanks to director Freddie
Francis's love of the building, this
horror-comedy made full use of
the house in its scenes.

JAWS

Set on the popular summer island of Martha's Vineyard, Steven Spielberg's water-bound action thriller ushered in the modern blockbuster—and waves of terror with it.

YEAR
1975

LOCATION
MASSACHUSETTS, US

Few movies have had such a huge cultural impact as *Jaws*. Steven Spielberg's tale of a great white terrorizing a small seaside town made generations of moviegoers petrified of the sea. Sharks became one of the scariest horror movie villains ever, despite barely featuring in the movie; composer John Williams's ominous two-note theme song was enough to send shivers down spines regardless. The movie's summer setting of a quaint seaside town didn't make things better; rather *Jaws* turned the typical vacation resort into the stuff of nightmares.

As in Peter Benchley's popular novel, *Jaws* is set in the fictional town of Amity.

While the author pictured this charming town on Long Island, Spielberg chose to shoot further north, in Edgartown. This seaside spot on Martha's Vineyard was ideal for its picturesque tourist town and shallow water. The shallow sea meant scenes with the mechanical shark—two contraptions named "Bruce"—could be filmed out of sight of land, without getting stranded in the deep.

As *Jaws* was the first major studio film to be shot on the ocean, it was inevitable things wouldn't go so swimmingly. The sharks suffered constant mechanical failures and looked so unconvincing that Spielberg was forced to reduce their screen time, much to the advantage of

Picturesque Edgartown, the fictional beach town of Amity

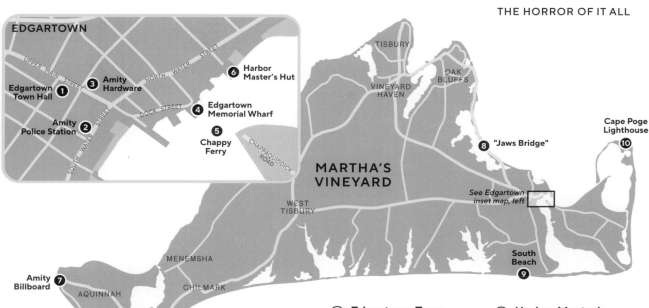

EDGARTOWN

- Edgartown Town Hall ①
- Amity Hardware ③
- Amity Police Station ②
- Harbor Master's Hut ⑥
- Edgartown Memorial Wharf ④
- Chappy Ferry ⑤

TISBURY

OAK BLUFFS

VINEYARD HAVEN

Cape Poge Lighthouse ⑩

"Jaws Bridge" ⑧

MARTHA'S VINEYARD

See Edgartown inset map, left

WEST TISBURY

South Beach ⑨

Amity Billboard ⑦

MENEMSHA

CHILMARK

AQUINNAH

the movie. To make matters worse, the weather turned, further damaging the sharks. As a result, filming dragged on for 159 days (instead of the intended 55), eating into the budget with as much ferocity as any great white. The extended shoot also meant that Robert Shaw and Richard Dreyfuss (whose relationship on set was far from cozy) were stuck together for triple the time expected. Their feud was so notorious that Richard's son, Ian, wrote a comedic play about it called *The Shark Is Broken*.

Against all odds, however, *Jaws* was completed and became the highest-grossing movie of all time—until *Star Wars (p166)* came out a few years later. Yet while *Jaws* did wonders for Spielberg's career, it's arguably not his favorite movie to look back on. You're far more likely to spot a shark off the coast of Martha's Vineyard than the director; he wouldn't recommend water-based filming to anyone.

① **Edgartown Town Hall**
This building stood in for Amity Town Hall, where shark hunter Quint introduces himself.

② **Amity Police Station**
Amity Police Station was located in a house at the corner of Davis Lane and South Water Street.

③ **Amity Hardware**
Amity Hardware was shown at 55 Main Street. Brodie stops by to buy materials to make "Beach Closed" signs here.

④ **Edgarton Memorial Wharf**
This is where Hooper comments that the ill-prepared sailors are "all gonna die."

⑤

Chappy Ferry
Chief Brodie and the mayor meet on this ferry to discuss the shark attacks.

⑥ **Harbor Master's Hut**
A tiger shark is strung up beside the Harbor Master's hut, located on Morse Street.

⑦ **Amity Billboard**
This graffitied billboard was installed at the Aquinnah Cliffs Overlook.

⑧ **"Jaws Bridge"**
Chief Brodie runs across this bridge (the "Jaws Bridge") between the Sengekontacket Pond and the ocean to rescue his son from the shark.

⑨

South Beach
The opening scene sees Chrissie take a swim, from which she never returns, off South Beach.

⑩ **Cape Poge Lighthouse**
The final scene of the survivors returning to shore was filmed on Chappaquiddick Island, near this lighthouse.

The Going-to-the-Sun Road, shown in the movie's opening scene

THE SHINING

The looming landscape of Glacier National Park provided the perfect introduction to this classic horror, which tells the tale of supernatural forces in the Overlook Hotel tormenting the Torrance family.

YEAR
1980

LOCATION
MONTANA AND OREGON, US

Stanley Kubrick's interpretation of Stephen King's *The Shining* may be one of the best psychological horrors ever made, but it was a turbulent affair behind the scenes. Filming lasted over a year due to the director's style of shooting—his methodical approach led to lengthy rehearsals and repeated takes. In demanding perfection from his cast, Kubrick crushed a Guinness World Record for most retakes of a scene with dialogue; it took a whopping 148 takes to nail the scene where young Danny Torrance and hotel chef Dick Hallorann discuss "the shine." Wendy swinging a bat at her husband, Jack, nabbed a close second with 127 takes.

These interior shots were all filmed at Elstree Studios, near Kubrick's home in England. The exterior shots, however, were the work of a crew in the US (Kubrick refused to fly). The opening Going-to-the-Sun Road footage was shot in the vast Glacier National Park, while the spooky Overlook hotel was played by Oregon's brooding Timberline Lodge *(p92)*. The hotel's management asked Kubrick not to depict room 217 (the room in the book) as they feared guests would be scared away, so the nonexistent room 237 was used instead. Funnily enough, today room 217 is the hotel's most requested—presumably there's no creepy woman in the bathtub.

IT

To create the quintessential small town from Stephen King's bestseller, production traveled just outside Toronto to the genteel Port Hope, the ideal setting for Pennywise's terrifying reign.

YEAR
2017, 2019

LOCATION
PORT HOPE, CANADA

According to the mythology of Stephen King's ancient evil, It reappears every 27 years. And just like clockwork, a two-part movie adaptation of King's book arrived in 2017—27 years after Tim Curry's clown terrorized viewers in the 1990 TV show.

King's story takes place in the fictional town of Derry, which was inspired by his hometown of Bangor, Maine. It made sense to shoot both movies in Bangor, with some locations even being scouted there, but budgetary reasons steered the movie elsewhere. The Canadian town of Port Hope, quaint and unassuming, was ultimately chosen as the setting for the trans-dimensional evil, It (to the children of Derry, It takes the form of villainous clown Pennywise).

To make It appear even more terrifying, the teens who played the Losers Club (Derry's resident group of outcasts) were kept at a distance from Bill Skarsgård (Pennywise) during much of the production. In scenes when they eventually encounter him, their horror-stricken reactions to Skarsgård's unnerving performance are genuine.

Happily, Port Hope isn't so terrifying, but it has embraced its links to the horror genre and offers *It* walking tours around the town's movie locations.

① Quality Meats
26 Walton Street is the location of Quality Meats. The butcher's back door and the ominous Derry mural can still be found down the neighboring alleyway.

④ Port Hope Town Hall
Port Hope Town Hall became Derry Public Library, where Ben researches the town's sinister history.

② The Capitol Theatre
The Capitol Theatre acts as Derry's local cinema. It's here that Richie plays arcade games in the first movie.

③ Port Hope Memorial Park
In *It Chapter Two*, Pennywise possesses a giant statue of the American lumberjack hero Paul Bunyan in this park.

AN AMERICAN WEREWOLF IN LONDON

London steals the show in this favorite creature feature, which sees its protagonist fleeing the menacing Yorkshire moors (well, Welsh mountains) only to find the capital a hotbed of horror.

YEAR
1981

LOCATION
ENGLAND; WALES

Director John Landis's 1980s classic *An American Werewolf In London* may largely take place in the capital, but that's not where the nightmare begins. The movie's doomed backpackers first encounter a werewolf on the Yorkshire moors—which are, in fact, played by the Black Mountains in Wales. Here, the village of Crickadern doubles as the fictional East Proctor; the exterior of the unwelcoming pub, the Slaughtered Lamb, was just an ordinary cottage in the village. The area might look particularly bleak on film, but the weather was surprising pleasant for Wales when the team started filming in February—Landis was forced to bring in rain machines to fit his vision.

Once the action moves to London, most of the landmarks you see on screen are real. Actor David Naughton (who played werewolf David Kessler) really did have to climb, naked, out of London Zoo's wolf enclosure. (Luckily for him, the wolves had just been fed and he had to do only one take.) And that poor commuter who falls prey to the beast really is running around Tottenham Court Road station.

Maybe the most impressive location used in the movie is Piccadilly Circus. No film crew had been given permission to close this central intersection before, but Landis had an ace up his sleeve. Having worked with the police on his previous movie *The Blues Brothers*, he knew how to get the force onside. He hosted a special private screening of *The Blues Brothers* for some 300 officers and the Metropolitan police eventually agreed to let him film here for a few snatched moments in the early morning.

Though London has changed a lot since Landis shot there, there is one filming location that looks more or less like it did in the '80s: Trafalgar Square. You'll have to turn your back on the modern Fourth Plinth and focus on Nelson's Column, but you'll still get to admire a part of London that David was too busy wolfing out to appreciate.

Tottenham Court Road station, a bad place to get chased by a werewolf

1

Tottenham Court Rd.

The late-night commuter scene was filmed at this Underground station, with the chase beginning at platform three.

2

Piccadilly Circus

David becomes a werewolf in an adult movie theater (no longer there) at this busy intersection.

4

Clink St.

The final scene was shot under the railroad bridge in Clink St. A false wall was added halfway to provide a definitive dead end.

5

Alex Price's Flat

Alex takes David back to her flat on Coleherne Road in Chelsea, now an eye-wateringly expensive place to live.

Trafalgar Square

After killing numerous people the night before, David tries and fails to get the police to arrest him in London's stately Trafalgar Square.

CAMDEN

Regent's Park

BLOOMSBURY

MARYLEBONE

LONDON

Tottenham Court Rd. **1**

COVENT GARDEN

CITY

BAYSWATER

SOHO

NOTTING HILL

Piccadilly Circus **2**

Hyde Park

MAYFAIR

River Thames

3 Trafalgar Square

4

Clink St.

5

SOUTHWARK

BERMONDSEY

ROTHERHITHE

BELGRAVIA

WESTMINSTER

Alex Price's **5** Flat

PIMLICO

3

CHELSEA

River Thames

Battersea Park

ON THE TRACKS

Werewolves, zombies, and gods alike have made the London Underground a star of the silver screen, and it's not the only one. Train stations around the world readily appear on film. All aboard!

PADDINGTON STATION, UK

Numerous London train stations have become fixtures of the big screen—think King's Cross in the *Harry Potter* movies (p74) or Waterloo in *The Bourne Ultimatum*—but few have popped up quite so often as Paddington. This bustling London spot has appeared in a mix of movies, from crime thriller *Layer Cake* (2004) to Richard Curtis's rom-com *About Time* (2013). And *Paddington* (p80), of course.

NEW YORK SUBWAY, US

There's always a homecoming or escape scene in need of a station, and New York's subway gives the London Underground a run for its money as the most seen subway on-screen. Key moments from action-thriller *The Warriors* (1979) were shot at Union Square and 72nd Street stations. Brooklyn's decommissioned Court Street station, meanwhile, was featured in *The French Connection (p198)* and *The Taking of Pelham 123* (1974).

JODHPUR, INDIA

For Wes Anderson's comedy-drama *The Darjeeling Limited* (2007), the train scenes were shot outside of the city of Jodhpur, making use of real-life, live rails; filming often had to pause to avoid the disturbance of passing trains. The train used in the movie had been painstakingly prepared by the production team; they replaced the interiors of ten coaches, and a track device was secured to the ceiling so that the camera could move without the use of a dolly.

GRAND CENTRAL TERMINAL, US

Having appeared in too many movies to count, it's clear that the vast concourse of Grand Central Terminal loves the camera. It was the scene of shots fired in both *Carlito's Way* (1993) and *I Am Legend* (2007), and it hosted a memorable waltz in Terry Gilliam's 1991 fever dream *The Fisher King*. Its best performance? That's arguably as Lex Luthor's lair in *Superman (p34)*.

CIOTAT STATION, FRANCE

Only one, 50-second movie has been recorded at this station near Marseilles, yet it has earned its place in cinema history. Shot by the Lumière brothers using their Cinematograph (a motion picture camera, printer, and projector) the short documents a steam train pulling into the station and marked the first time a train appeared in a movie.

1 Paddington Bear statue at his namesake station

2 A New York subway platform

3 The three brothers racing to catch the train in *The Darjeeling Limited*

4 The main concourse at Grand Central Terminal

5 The working Ciotat station, near Marseilles

1

2

3

4

5

THE EXORCIST

Often dubbed the scariest movie ever made, the tale of Regan McNeil's possession by an ancient demon turned its strait-laced Georgetown setting into the stuff of nightmares.

YEAR
1973

LOCATION
US; IRAQ

Movies don't always stay true to their source material settings, but director William Friedkin's terrifying adaptation of *The Exorcist* did. Following the horror novel (written by William Peter Blatty), *The Exorcist* takes place in Georgetown, Washington, DC. The author purposely chose this prim neighborhood to contrast with the book's harrowing subject matter: the demonic possession of Regan McNeil. During preliminary movie discussions, Blatty even rejected an initial director for wanting to shift the action to Salem, the infamous (if not clichéd) witch capital in Massachusetts..

Numerous *Exorcist* landmarks can be found around Georgetown today. The McNeils' home, where Regan's worried mother brings priests to exorcise the demon possessing her daughter, is located at 3600 Prospect Street. Just next door is the movie's most famous location: the narrow staircase Father Damien Karras falls down. (Fortunately for his stuntman, rubber padding was added to the steps to cushion his fall.) These infamously steep stairs (now called The Exorcist Steps) already had a creepy reputation—locals had previously called them the Hitchcock Steps.

While much of *The Exorcist* takes place in DC, the movie's chilling prologue was shot around Mosul, in Iraq. In Blatty's novel, it's here that a priest unearths an artifact representing the ancient demon Pazuzu, which then possesses Regan. Determined to stay true to the book, Friedkin headed to Iraq, unfazed

The legendary Exorcist Steps, a must-visit for horror movie fans

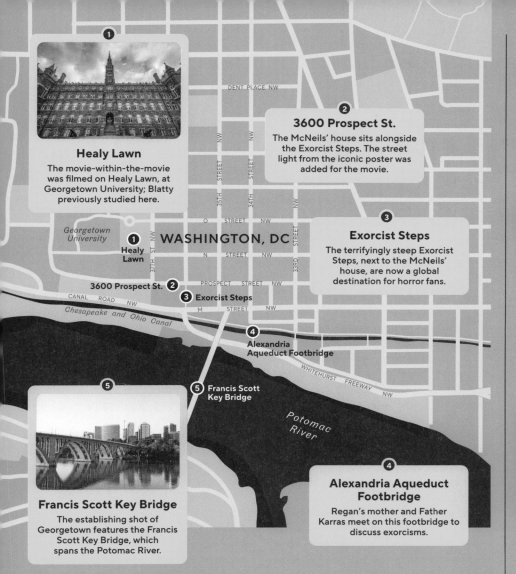

Healy Lawn

The movie-within-the-movie was filmed on Healy Lawn, at Georgetown University; Blatty previously studied here.

3600 Prospect St.

The McNeils' house sits alongside the Exorcist Steps. The street light from the iconic poster was added for the movie.

Exorcist Steps

The terrifyingly steep Exorcist Steps, next to the McNeils' house, are now a global destination for horror fans.

Francis Scott Key Bridge

The establishing shot of Georgetown features the Francis Scott Key Bridge, which spans the Potomac River.

Alexandria Aqueduct Footbridge

Regan's mother and Father Karras meet on this footbridge to discuss exorcisms.

① Healy Lawn
② 3600 Prospect St.
③ Exorcist Steps
④ Alexandria Aqueduct Footbridge
⑤ Francis Scott Key Bridge

Georgetown University
WASHINGTON, DC
Chesapeake and Ohio Canal
Potomac River
WHITEHURST FREEWAY NW
CANAL ROAD NW
DENT PLACE NW

FAMOUS STAIRCASES ON SCREEN

The Exorcist Steps might have the fright factor, but they're not the only stairs to have gained fame via the big screen.

ROCKY

Philadelphia Museum of Art, Philadelphia, US

Thousands of visitors copy Rocky's ascent of these 72 steps every year. A statue of the boxing underdog can be found here, too.

- - - - - - - - - - - - - - - - - -

THE JOKER

Anderson Avenue, 167th St, New York, US

Joaquin Phoenix's Joker whimsically dances down this Bronx-based step street. The scene became an instant internet meme and the steps are now a tourist attraction.

- - - - - - - - - - - - - - - - - -

GAME OF THRONES

Jesuit Staircase, Dubrovnik, Croatia

There's nothing noticeably "shameful" about this gorgeous Baroque staircase where Cersei Lannister is publicly punished.

by the country's civil unrest and sweltering temperatures. Poor diplomatic relations between the US and Iraq, however, meant that the director himself was in charge of negotiating the filming arrangements. The Iraqi officials allowed him to film as long as he employed Iraqi workers and taught filmmaking classes to locals.

For a movie so notorious upon release (audiences fainting in the theater wasn't uncommon), the making of *The Exorcist* seemed fittingly cursed. Aside from the issues faced in Iraq, several cast members suffered severe injuries while on set and mysterious fires broke out. One burned the interior of the McNeil house (a set in New York). Regan's bedroom, however—which was kept well below freezing to show the actors' breath—was creepily left intact.

Interestingly, Blatty never thought of *The Exorcist* as a horror story. But those who struggle to shake the image of Regan's twisting head will surely beg to differ.

MIDSOMMAR

There aren't many horror movies that look like *Midsommar*. Forget dark alleyways and spooky old houses, Ari Aster's sophomore feature, which was mostly shot in the Hungarian countryside, is a sun-soaked nightmare.

YEAR
2019

LOCATION
BUDAPEST, HUNGARY

As break-up movies go, director Ari Aster's *Midsommar* might just be the most traumatic (and, hopefully, the least relatable). This contemporary folk horror follows the barely together couple Dani and Christian to a Swedish midsummer festival. Events take a twisted turn, however, when the pair discover they've stumbled right into a sinister pagan cult, and one with a penchant for human sacrifices.

Though *Midsommar* is set in Sweden, production headed to Hungary. While the country is a hit with movie crews for its generous tax incentives (*Black Widow* *[p29]* and *Dune* *[p158]* were shot here, too), aesthetically the leafy suburbs of

Budapest provided the perfect natural backdrop for Aster's pagan festival. Working with production designer Henrik Svensson, the director spent two months searching for the ideal field to host the movie's sinister event, eventually settling near an airfield in Budakeszi (just a 20-minute drive from the city center). Svensson then spent two more months building a Swedish-inspired commune on the site. The buildings' painted interior walls were inspired by the carefully decorated farmhouses of Hälsingland, Sweden, which are now a World Heritage Site. Away from the set, nearby Régi kőbánya ("old quarry") was chosen for the movie's pivotal *ättestupa* suicide ritual.

At the end of *Midsommar*'s production, the festival set was removed and the cult's temple, as in the movie, was burned to the ground. Visiting the field in Budakeszi may, therefore, appeal only to hardcore fans. Those eager to revel in a real midsummer festival are in luck: celebrations take place in Sweden and are much friendlier than in the movie.

Bucolic Budakeszi,
the ideal location for a
midsummer festival

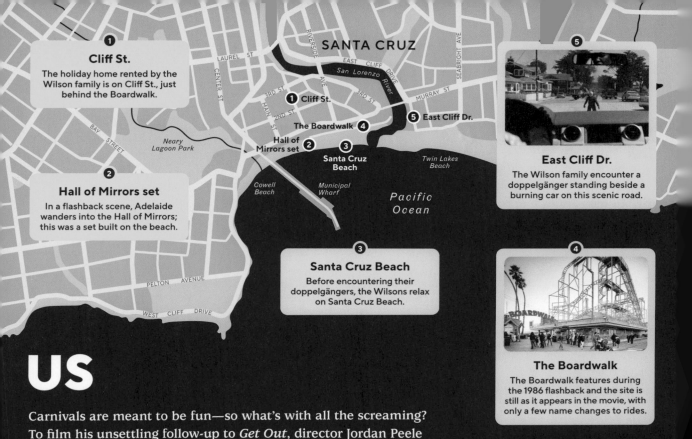

SANTA CRUZ

① Cliff St.
The holiday home rented by the Wilson family is on Cliff St., just behind the Boardwalk.

① Cliff St.

The Boardwalk **④**

② Hall of Mirrors set
In a flashback scene, Adelaide wanders into the Hall of Mirrors; this was a set built on the beach.

Hall of Mirrors set **②**

⑤ East Cliff Dr.

Santa Cruz Beach **③**

Neary Lagoon Park

Cowell Beach

Municipal Wharf

Twin Lakes Beach

Pacific Ocean

⑤ East Cliff Dr.
The Wilson family encounter a doppelgänger standing beside a burning car on this scenic road.

③ Santa Cruz Beach
Before encountering their doppelgängers, the Wilsons relax on Santa Cruz Beach.

④ The Boardwalk
The Boardwalk features during the 1986 flashback and the site is still as it appears in the movie, with only a few name changes to rides.

US

Carnivals are meant to be fun—so what's with all the screaming? To film his unsettling follow-up to *Get Out*, director Jordan Peele headed to a historic amusement park in California.

YEAR
2019

LOCATION
CALIFORNIA, US

Appearances can never be trusted in Jordan Peele's movies: the more familiar something appears, the scarier it'll probably turn out to be. And so it was in his haunting movie *Us*, with the sunny Santa Cruz Beach Boardwalk the setting for all sorts of horrors.

Peele always knew that the movie would be both set and shot in California, in a homage to an icon of the horror genre. "Alfred Hitchcock is one of my favorite directors," he told *Fandom*, "And the West Coast beach vibe of Santa Cruz reminded me of *The Birds* and *Vertigo*." Choosing the area was a no-brainer, with the most cinematic fair on the West Coast. Think it looks

familiar? It's featured in plenty of movies, most memorably in Joel Schumacher's 1987 vampire romp *The Lost Boys*. Peele even throws in a reference to the shared location in *Us*, with Adelaide's mother remarking "they're filming something by the carousel." Remember Kiefer Sutherland's vampire villain and his gang pushing their way through the carousel horses? That's the carousel she's talking about.

If you're visiting the boardwalk today, you might be disappointed to hear that the Hall of Mirrors was created just for the movie. Thankfully, The Haunted Castle, a monster-packed boardwalk ride seen briefly in the movie, offers its own spooky beachside thrills.

DON'T LOOK NOW

Nicolas Roeg's adaptation of Daphne DuMaurier's short story is a supernatural thriller that draws much of its gothic atmosphere from its setting: the sparsely populated, wintry streets of Venice.

YEAR
1973

LOCATION
**VENICE, ITALY;
ENGLAND**

Picture Venice, and sun-soaked plazas and pretty canals come to mind. Not so in *Don't Look Now*. Director Nicolas Roeg's unsettling chiller shows viewers a more haunting version of this Italian city.

Following a prelude in Hertfordshire, England, where the young daughter of John and Laura Baxter tragically drowns, *Don't Look Now* travels to Italy's most eye-catching city. But Roeg isn't focused on Venice's obvious beauty; the director shies away from the city's landmarks, choosing to shoot off the tourist trail and during the winter instead. With the crowds dispersed and the mist rolling in, Venice gains a claustrophobic and ghostly air. Lonely alleyways become an unnerving maze and supernatural forces seem to linger around the couple.

The Venetian sights Roeg chooses to focus on are all low-key, local places. The church John Baxter repairs as he deals with the death of his daughter, for example, is the 12th-century San Nicolò dei Mendicoli. In a happy coincidence, the church itself was in a state of disrepair at the time of filming, and the scaffolding seen in the movie was already in place when shooting began. As fans will remember, it's in this church that John Baxter nearly falls to his death. This stunt wasn't exactly straightforward, but that didn't seem to faze actor Donald Sutherland; that's him you see on screen, not a double.

Sutherland's luck may have held up but John's soon runs out. The movie's ending sees him searching the dimly lit alleyways for someone he believes to be his daughter, only to find more death and tragedy at the end of the maze. Unsurprisingly, this wasn't the sunny image Venetians wanted of their city, and many were afraid *Don't Look Now* would scare visitors away. Their fears were entirely unfounded, however; the overtouristed streets of today are a far cry from the movie's eerie quietness.

The Chiesa di San Stae on the Grand Canal, seen in the movie's credits

The Hotel Gabrielli, used for the Baxters' Venice residence, the Europa Hotel

② Basilica dei Santi Giovanni e Paolo
When Laura lights a candle here, John remarks that he doesn't like the church. This exchange was copied from a real conversation between the two actors.

VENICE

CAMPO DELLA PESCHIERA

PIAZZALE ROMA

CAMPO SAN POLO

Canal Grande

② Basilica dei Santi Giovanni e Paolo

③ Palazzo Grimani

San Nicolò dei Mendicoli
①

CAMPO SANTA MARGHERITA

CAMPO SANT' ANGELO

CAMPO SANTO STEFANO

PIAZZA SAN MARCO

④ Waterfront

⑤ Hotel Gabrielli

Canale di San Marco

③

⑤

San Nicolò dei Mendicoli
Chiesa di San Nicolò dei Mendicoli, the 12th-century church John is renovating, is no longer in a state of disrepair and is now open to visitors.

Palazzo Grimani
The tragic last scene takes place in the Palazzo Grimani. The building was abandoned at the time of filming but is now a museum.

⑤ Hotel Gabrielli
The Hotel Gabrielli was used as the exterior of the Europa Hotel, where the couple stay during their time in Venice.

④ Waterfront
While exploring the city, the couple walk along the waterfront between Hotel Gabrielli and San Marco.

5

CRIME AND PUNISHMENT

Stories of criminal misdeeds, whether a shiver-inducing true crime or a perfectly plotted whodunit, have long captured our imagination. And with their explosive car chases, violent heists, and scheming felons, crime movies have the ability to captivate and shock in equal measure.

But crime features also remind us that character and place are inseparable. Every criminal needs a base for their crimes, just as every detective needs a refuge from which to survey the scene: perhaps it's a drug lab in a run-down RV, the foothills of Sicily, or the deserts of the American West. And when solving the crime and catching the felon involve negotiating the intricate puzzle of the crime scene, locations have just as much to say as the characters who exist in them.

BREAKING BAD AND BETTER CALL SAUL

Breaking Bad and prequel series *Better Call Saul* turned Albuquerque's local businesses and surrounding landscapes into TV pilgrimage sites, drawing fans far into the desert in search of the franchise's wild world.

YEAR
2008–2013
2015–2022

LOCATION
NEW MEXICO, US

Little known to global audiences, the city of Albuquerque, New Mexico, skyrocketed to fame when it became the home of Walter White, *Breaking Bad*'s chemistry teacher turned crime lord. Two years after *Breaking Bad* ended, fans were summoned back to the desert for the critically acclaimed prequel series *Better Call Saul*.

Production of *Breaking Bad* was originally intended for the Californian city of Riverside, but tax rebates led producer Vince Gilligan (creator of *The X Files*) to New Mexico instead. Since then, Albuquerque has become synonymous with the extended *Breaking Bad* universe—so much so that family homes and other everyday staples have become booming local attractions. The "White" residence has seen many inadvisable pizza-throwing attempts onto its roof while the fully functioning Mister Car Wash is open for business. You can even purchase some of White's illegal product at the local store (the meth used in the show is actually rock candy).

Better Call Saul only further cemented Albuquerque in the world of *Breaking Bad*. Originally planned as a weekly comedy half hour, the prequel series instead became a dramatic exploration of lawyer Jimmy McGill's tumultuous world, before his transformation into the sleazier Saul Goodman. With Jimmy an Albuquerque resident, the series saw a return to some of the locations made famous by *Breaking Bad*. The vast scrubland of the Canoncito Indian Reserve, for example, is both the backdrop for Jimmy and his associate Mike Ehrmantraut's dehydrated trek through the desert, and the setting for Walt and Jesse's first cooking session

DEVIL IN THE DETAIL

Both series went to great lengths to ensure their scripts were accurate. Donna Nelson, a professor of organic chemistry, was on hand to check *Breaking Bad* for scientific accuracy. Meanwhile, one writer had to rewatch all 62 *Breaking Bad* episodes before each *Better Call Saul* season to check for continuity details.

Canoncito Indian Reservation, a quiet spot for a cookout

(just to the west of Trail 7089), among countless other scenes in *Breaking Bad*.

Better Call Saul did introduce fans to some new locations, including Jimmy's law firm, which is set in the real-life Day Spa & Nail salon (still complete with his favorite massage chairs). Hamlin, Hamlin & McGill's exterior and interior offices were split across two buildings; they may have been a short walk from each other, but filming still proved a headache for the show's location manager, who had to deal with two separate owners.

Though both series dwell on the trouble beneath suburbia's surface, they never forget to show the beauty of Albuquerque's surrounding landscape. In fact, such was the allure of the sweeping desert dunes and blue carpet skies that Bryan Cranston (aka Walter White) has since taken up residence in "The Land of Enchantment." So be careful who you open your door to … you might come face to face with "Heisenberg" himself.

(1) **Canoncito Indian Reservation**
Featuring in *Breaking Bad*'s opening scene, and throughout the franchise, this reserve became a go-to setting.

(2) **Pan American Building**
The Hamlin, Hamlin & McGill law firm's exterior was this building on 100 Sun Ave NE.

(3) **US-285 and Spur Ranch Rd.**
The train heist in *Breaking Bad*'s fifth season episode "Dead Freight" was shot in this location.

(4) **9800 Montgomery Blvd NE**
Saul Goodman opened his office here; the building now houses a bar.

(5)

Mister Car Wash
Walt and Skyler launder money through the A1A Car Wash, the real-life Mister Car Wash, in *Breaking Bad*.

(6) **Day Spa & Nail**
Jimmy's backroom law firm was set at this salon in *Better Call Saul*.

(7) **Crossroads Motel**
"The Crystal Palace," as Hank Schrader calls it, appears throughout *Breaking Bad*.

(8)

Twisters
The Twisters fast food chain on 4275 Isleta Blvd SW became Los Pollos Hermanos, the front for Gus Fring's crime operation in both series.

(9) **Convention Center**
Mike Ehrmantraut's parking booth is under Marquette Ave NW Rd, by the Convention Center.

(10) **Candy Lady**
You can buy the rock candy used as crystal meth in the show from this sweet shop.

TWIN PEAKS

David Lynch and Mark Frost's murder-mystery series *Twin Peaks* was filmed in and around the Snoqualmie Valley, a bucolic town in the Evergreen State with towering trees and damn fine coffee.

YEAR
1990–1991, 2017

LOCATION
WASHINGTON, US

The cinematic worlds of David Lynch resemble the off-kilter texture of dreams. On the surface, his movies reflect the humdrum details of everyday life, but look more closely and you'll see something bizarre happening beneath the perfect veneer of small-town America. While he first explored this idea in his 1986 mystery thriller *Blue Velvet*, he was convinced to revisit it for the TV series *Twin Peaks* at the urging of his agent.

Lynch and cocreator Mark Frost began by drawing a schematic for the fictional town of Twin Peaks. This map initially took precedence over the array of quirky characters eventually involved in the show's murder-mystery storyline, emphasizing the importance of setting for the two filmmakers from the get-go.

Twin Peaks was originally fixed to take place in North Dakota, but Lynch and Frost soon realized the plains lacked the mystery of America's northwest forests. At the suggestion of a friend, they drove out to Snoqualmie Falls and, upon their arrival, immediately knew that they'd found their setting. Here, the lush vistas of Washington state

Salish Lodge and Spa

While trying to solve Laura Palmer's murder, Cooper stays at the Great Northern Hotel. The Salish Lodge and Spa was used for the exterior.

Snoqualmie Falls

These falls appear in *Twin Peaks'* opening credits. In the series, they're known as White Trail Falls.

Dirtfish Rally School

The Twin Peaks Sheriff's Department is now a driving school, but the building is still recognizable.

Reinig Bridge

Ronette Pulaski walks across this bridge the day after Laura Palmer's death. The railroad tracks have gone and the bridge is now pedestrianized.

Kiana Lodge
67 km (42 miles)

Salish Lodge and Spa ①
Snoqualmie Falls ②

③ Dirtfish Rally School

④ Reinig Bridge

⑤ "Welcome to Twin Peaks"

SNOQUALMIE RIDGE

SNOQUALMIE

WA-202

Snoqualmie River

WA-202

I-90

WASHINGTON

Twede's Cafe ⑥ NORTH BEND

Kiana Lodge

Laura Palmer's body is discovered on the beach outside this Poulsbo venue—the giant log is still there.

"Welcome to Twin Peaks"

The "Welcome to Twin Peaks" sign was placed on the Southeast Reinig Road, with Mount Si visible in the background.

Twede's Cafe

The original series used a studio set for the interior scenes of the Double R Diner, but 2017's season 3 remodeled Twede's Cafe and filmed on site.

fortuitously matched the locations from their script and schematic, with the Snoqualmie Valley really bringing the fictional town of Twin Peaks to life. Frost and Lynch were delighted to find specific places for their feature-length pilot—among them a typical diner, a sheriff's station, a roadhouse, and a sawmill—all within the vicinity, as if it were meant to be. After the pilot was complete, much of the series was shot on sound stages, but the still-operating Salish Lodge and Spa and

The thundering Snoqualmie Falls, star of the show's opening credits

stunning Snoqualmie Falls are forever immortalized in the memorable opening credits of the series.

It's hard to imagine Agent Dale Cooper driving into any other town, winding down the windows to breathe in the fresh air. Those peaks still stand, shrouded in fog, and roadside cafés still serve Cooper-approved cherry pie.

LYNCH FILM LOCATIONS

David Lynch's films may feel surreal, but they're set in the most ordinary places.

BLUE VELVET
(1986)

The Carolina Apartments in Wilmington, North Carolina, double as the home of lounge singer Dorothy Vallens in this hypnotic noir.

MULHOLLAND DRIVE
(2001)

The film's climactic sequence features Rebekah Del Rio lip-syncing inside Club Silencio. The scene was shot at the Tower Theater in Los Angeles, which also played the Fireman's house in *Twin Peaks'* season 3.

BABY DRIVER

Early in development, *Baby Driver* moved its action from Los Angeles to Atlanta. Fortunately for this up-tempo heist caper, the so-called Hollywood of the South hit all the right notes.

YEAR
2017

LOCATION
GEORGIA, US

To some extent, *Baby Driver* could have been shot anywhere. Edgar Wright's lively crime thriller isn't so much staged in a location as it is laid along the bars of a song. The infectious jukebox soundtrack was a world unto itself; every single scene and car chase seemed to dance to its rhythms.

Perhaps this is why Wright was willing to abandon the script's original setting. Another (more practical) reason was the tax incentives offered by Georgia, which helped steer the film crew toward central Atlanta. These financial incentives have made the American city a haven for movies and TV shows, though it's usually used as a stand-in for other locales. For Wright, this wasn't an option; he rewrote the script, inserting a number of Atlanta-specific references and even a geographically accurate car chase. It was the perfect place, of course, given Atlanta's storied music scene and famed love of cars. Local businesses like Octane Coffee, Criminal Records, and Goodfella's Pizza and Wings were given their dues, while downtown, the historical buildings and freeway ramps provided a striking backdrop to the high-stakes antics of getaway driver Baby and a crew of bank robbers.

Baby Driver would have surely been fine if it had filmed in LA, but Atlanta may have just given the film its soul.

The crew spark a shoot-out at Pullman Yards, in reality an entertainment hub

NO COUNTRY FOR OLD MEN

Joel and Ethan Coen's thriller—which follows Llewelyn Moss as he flees the clutches of a psychopathic hit man—makes full use of the barren border towns and seedy motels of America's new wild west.

YEAR
2007

LOCATION
NEW MEXICO AND TEXAS, US

Long associated with the lawless criminals and cowboys of early westerns, the sweeping desert plains and remote frontier towns of the American West provided the perfect backdrop for this enthralling thriller.

Though Cormac McCarthy's source novel is set in Texas, the Coen Brothers' neo-western—starring Josh Brolin as Llewelyn Moss and an award-winning Javier Bardem as the terrifying killer Anton Chigurh—was largely filmed in Las Vegas, New Mexico (not Sin City). With its array of historic buildings, the characterful city looks little changed from the frontier era, making it the perfect stand-in for the Texas border towns of Eagle Pass and Del Rio. It's here that Moss closely escapes Chigurh in the city's Plaza Hotel and the Regal Inn.

Texas played its part, however. Moss's fateful discovery of a botched drug deal was shot in the vast Big Bend National Park, in the state's west. Despite the area having little cinematic fame, the team were coincidentally sharing it with director Paul Thomas Anderson. The horizon smoke wafting from his set of *There Will Be Blood* (2007) forced the Coen Brothers to cut their filming short.

With such powerful performances by Brolin and Bardem, *No Country For Old Men* became a landmark neo-western—perhaps doing little to improve cinema's image of the wild west in the process.

Regal Inn
Moss hides the money he's stolen at the Regal Inn motel on the CanAm Highway.

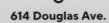
Regal Inn

2
614 Douglas Ave.
Chigurh helps himself to medical supplies from the Mike Zoss Pharmacy, shot at this address.

Plaza Hotel
On-the-run Moss stays at the Eagle Pass hotel (the historic Plaza Hotel); it's here that he narrowly escapes Chigurh.

East University Bridge
A fake border station required the installation of a 50,000 lb (23-ton) steel structure here.

LAS VEGAS

East University Bridge

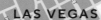
614 Douglas Ave.

Plaza Hotel

BACK TO THE FUTURE
PART III (1990) ▶

A love letter to the western, this movie sees Marty travel back in time to 1885. His arrival in the fictional town of Hill Valley begins in this scenic setting.

NATIONAL LAMPOON'S
VACATION (1983)

In this comedy, the Griswold family finds themselves stranded in Monument Valley after a crash. Clark, the dad, gets lost here trying to find help.

MONUMENT VALLEY

Rising above expansive desert plains, the sandstone towers of Monument Valley have made many an appearance on the silver screen—especially in classic westerns.

Located in the Navajo Nation Reservation on the Utah-Arizona border, this otherworldly valley is awe-inspiring. Towering buttes rise out of the flat, red sand, some soaring an incredible 1,000 ft (300 m) high. These ancient sandstone pillars, whipped into shape by the elements, have long been a staple of wild west movies, their rugged forms providing the perfect backdrop for the genre's whip-wielding cowboys.

The superhero movies of their day, westerns dominated the box office for over 50 years from the 1920s, with Monument Valley playing a starring role in many movies. Director John Ford in particular loved the area; he shot nine movies here, many featuring western icon John Wayne. While the valley has since appeared in other movies, including *Forrest Gump* (1994) and *Transformers: Age of Extinction* (2014), its vast plains will be forever synonymous with cowboy movies.

FORREST GUMP (1994) ▶
This movie remains a well-loved classic. After running across the states for over three years, Forrest Gump's marathon comes to an end on a long stretch of road that cuts through the valley.

STAGECOACH (1939)
Starring a young John Wayne, this was the first-ever movie that John Ford shot in Monument Valley. Here, a group of travelers make their way through the area's dusty desert landscape.

PEAKY BLINDERS

Set in the Birmingham district of Small Heath, this period gangster series ventured to cities across England to recreate its interwar industrial vibe, with Liverpool, Manchester, and, of course, Birmingham playing their part.

YEAR
2013–2022

LOCATION
ENGLAND

Was *Peaky Blinders* ever really Brummie enough? Throughout its run, this slick, addictive crime drama (following the eponymous Birmingham gang) faced this question on a semi-regular basis. The problem wasn't just the varying accents—which cast members insisted were period-accurate—but the look and feel of the city itself. As it turns out, there was a good reason for this. "The Birmingham we needed to recreate […] doesn't exist anymore," said producer Frith Tiplady, alluding

to the terrible bombing the Midlands city had faced during the Blitz. To approximate the gritty industrialized sprawl of 20th-century Birmingham, the show had to make do with other English locales.

Liverpool's many historic buildings and traditional terraced streets made it a favorite filming location during the show's run. Tommy Shelby's Watery Lane turf, for example, was set on Powis Street (now completely unrecognizable due to redevelopment), in the Toxteth area, while Aunt Polly's Birmingham home was shot in the time-warped village of Port Sunlight, not far from Liverpool. Nearby Ellesmere Port stood in for Camden Lock during the gang's forays into London, while Bolton's Le Mans Crescent was used for rival Sabini's jazz haunt, the Eden Club.

But *Peaky Blinders* is, of course, rooted in the city of Birmingham. The Black Country Living Museum, in the town of Dudley, proved an invaluable resource; Charlie Strong's yard was filmed by the canal arm here and Ada and Freddie's secret meeting place is located along the bridge. Still, fans of the show hoping to roam the industrialized streets of Birmingham will have to contend with the haunts of the real-life Peaky Blinders rather than the disreputable Shelbys.

Whether or not *Peaky*'s vision of Small Heath was ever fastidiously accurate is, for most, beside the point. The series winningly evoked a bygone Birmingham rife with violence and melodrama—and, for viewers, a whole lot of thrills.

The Black Country Living Museum's canal network, a favorite *Peaky* haunt

Bolton

The gang's visit to the Eden Club in London, in season 2 episode 1, was shot at Le Mans Crescent.

Manchester

The horse fair in season 2 was filmed in the Victoria Baths in Manchester.

Liverpool

Liverpool's Powis Street played Tommy's Watery Lane home, while Formby Beach appears in the season 4 finale.

Port Sunlight

A house in Port Sunlight, on the Wirral, was Aunt Polly's Sutton Coldfield home.

Arley Hall and Gardens

As Tommy Shelby gains power and status, he moves from Small Heath to this estate in season 3.

Black Country Living Museum

This open-air village was home to many locations in the series, including Charlie's yard.

Blackpool
Preston
Bradford
Leeds
Irish Sea
Wigan
Bolton
Doncaster
Liverpool
Manchester
Sheffield
Warrington
Port Sunlight
Arley Hall and Gardens

ENGLAND

Stoke-on-Trent
Derby

Shrewsbury
WALES
Leicester
Wolverhampton
Black Country Living Museum
Birmingham

Worcester

THE GODFATHER

Arguably cinema's greatest crime saga, Francis Ford Coppola's Oscar-winning masterpiece wouldn't be the same without the gritty streets of New York City and the sun-soaked landscapes of Sicily.

Calvary Cemetery, Don Corleone's burial place

YEAR
1972

LOCATION
NEW YORK, US; SICILY

Based on Mario Puzo's bestselling novel, *The Godfather* chronicles the criminal exploits of the fictional Corleone family. It's an eventful saga, and behind-the-scenes equally so. As soon as Mafia bosses heard about a potential adaptation of Puzo's crime novel, they expressed their unhappiness (apparently a dead rat was placed on Paramount executive Robert Evans's bed as a warning). To avert more threats, newbie producer Albert S. Ruddy contacted Mafia boss Joe Colombo. Through letters and a personal meeting, Ruddy assured Colombo the word "Mafia" would never appear; it doesn't.

The drama didn't stop there. Evans's decision to hire Francis Ford Coppola, a director with a bumpy track record, went against the studio's wishes. But Coppola's creative touch proved a success. Passionate about shooting on location, the director shot 90 percent of the action in New York City, immersing the story in the Big Apple. For the scenes outside New York, he headed to the picturesque town of Savoca in Sicily. Here, he shot in the Chiesa di San Nicolò (where Michael Corleone and Apollonia get married) and Bar Vitelli (where the match is arranged). The town remains a huge draw for fans of the movie, yet it's the historical streets of New York that truly cemented *The Godfather* as a classic of American cinema.

GOODFELLAS

Goodfellas reveals a seedy and corrupt New York City whose grime and glamour makes it the perfect setting for this gangster-origin story.

YEAR
1990

LOCATION
NEW YORK, US

In the summer of 1989, director Martin Scorsese used the cinematic splendor of his native New York City to create one of the finest gangster movies ever made. Adapted from the book *Wiseguy*—written by Nicholas Pileggi and based on the life of gangster Henry Hill—*Goodfellas* is at turns dark, dazzling, and dangerous—adjectives that could easily be applied to the city itself.

In Scorsese's quest for authenticity, getting the details right was essential. While this meant using Italian tailors and proper Italian food (made by the director's mother, no less), it also meant hiring gangsters as actors and consultants. Keeping track of props became a full time job—at one point fake $100 bills briefly entered general circulation. Incidentally, Robert De Niro (who played gangster Jimmy Conway) didn't like the feeling of fake money, so he used $5,000 of his own cash in his scenes.

Many of the movie's locations have since been lost to gentrification, such as the Copacabana nightclub where the one-take steadicam shot was filmed. Yet one place remains intact: Neir's Tavern, in Queens, where the Christmas party was filmed. It's embraced its *Goodfellas* fame with a themed menu—try the Pink Cadillac burger if you're feeling bold.

 ①

St. Regis Hotel
The luxurious St. Regis Hotel is seen regularly in the movie; it's notably where Michael Corleone and his wife Kay stay in the city.

② **Calvary Cemetery**
Don Corleone's funeral was shot at Calvary Cemetery in Queens. The coordinates of his grave are 40.734, −73.928.

③ **St. Patrick's Cathedral**
Michael and Kay's son's christening takes place inside this landmark.

④

Radio City Music Hall
Michael and Kay see *The Bells of St. Mary's* at this venue.

THE THIRD MAN

Director Carol Reed's genre-defining thriller explores the shadowy streets of postwar Vienna, turning the city's subterranean spaces into a hotbed of scheming con men and cunning racketeers.

YEAR
1949

LOCATION
VIENNA, AUSTRIA

An icon of film noir, *The Third Man* made full use of the genre's trademarks: moody lighting, morally ambiguous characters, and a notable absence of clear heroes. In keeping with Graham Greene's book, on which the movie is based, director Carol Reed set his thriller in Vienna, just after World War II. Then an occupied and divided city, the Austrian capital is seen on screen as a place of ravaged beauty and political unrest. Such was the power of Greene's screenplay and Reed's use of Viennese landmarks in shoots that the city practically became a character in itself.

The Third Man follows American writer Holly Martins as he investigates the death of his mysterious friend Harry Lime. As Lime's death becomes more and more suspicious, and viewers learn about his dabbling in the black market of vital medicines, the search through Vienna's cobbled alleyways intensifies. The hunt culminates with the iconic appearance of Lime himself, a scene memorably shot in the front doorway of the Schreyvogelgasse 8.

It's upon Vienna's moonlit roads that Reed's atmospheric filmmaking shines, but even the movie's daytime settings possess an air of tension. One of the most famous scenes was shot on the Viennese Giant Ferris Wheel (Wiener Riesenrad), in Prater Park. This traditional site of family fun becomes the stage for Lime's haunting speech (partly devised by Orson Welles, who played him), in which he evokes the terror and bloodshed of the ruthless

The Viennese Giant Ferris Wheel, a famous feature of *The Third Man*

① Schreyvogelgasse 8
Here, Holly Martins first finds Harry Lime, dramatically spotlit in the building's doorway.

② Wiener Prater
The Ferris wheel in this park is where Lime and Martin have their infamous conversation.

LEOPOLDSTADT

PRATER-STERN

Wiener Prater ②

ROOSEVELT-PLATZ

Donaukanal

FRANZ-JOSEFS-KAI

SCHOTTENRING

TABORSTRASSE

PRATERSTR.

Schreyvogelgasse 8 ①

HERRENGASSE

AM HOF

RATHAUS-PLATZ

LANDESGERICHTSSTR.

Volks-garten

INNERE STADT

ROTENTURMSTR.

STEPHANS-PLATZ

SCHULERSTR.

STUBENRING

Palais Pallavicini ⑥

KÄRNTNER STRASSE

VIENNA

Burg-garten

Stadt-park

MESSEPLATZ

SCHUBERTRING

SCHWARZEN-BERGPLATZ

REISNERSTRASSE

MARIAHILFER STR.

Girardipark ⑤

KARLS-PLATZ

RENNWEG

LINKE WIENZEILE

RECHTE WIENZEILE

Dritte Mann Museum ④

PRINZ-EUGEN-STRASSE

WIEDEN

Belvedere

→ Wiener Zentralfriedhof ③
6 km (4 miles)

LANDSTRASSER GÜRTEL

③ Wiener Zentralfriedhof
The movie's melancholy ending takes place at this cemetery, which is the final resting place of Lime.

④ Dritte Mann Museum
The Third Man Museum details the famous movie and how it reflected life in postwar Vienna.

⑥

Palais Pallavicini
This gorgeous building in Josefsplatz is a stand-in for Lime's apartment; he apparently gets hit by a truck outside it.

⑤ Girardipark
Lime flees into the sewers through a distinctive star-shaped access plate in Girardipark.

Borgias, a noble family known for their role in Italian politics. In true noir style, even the brightest corners of the city serve as reminders of the darkness lurking in the human heart.

Reed used Vienna's dank sewers for the movie's thrilling climactic chase, a physical descent into the city's imagined underworld. There are now an array of walking tours that take fans into this sewer system, as well as a host of other locations in the movie.

Although this portrayal of Vienna was not, initially, warmly received by locals, Reed's movie has since become a defining image of the city. A visit to see the Baroque grandeur of the streets, contrasting perfectly with the buried tunnels lying below, is now a ritual for many fans of classic noir cinema.

SHERLOCK

This charismatic TV series reintroduced the world to everybody's favorite British detective, with many of his case-cracking adventures unsurprisingly set in the very heart of London.

YEAR
2010–2017

LOCATION
ENGLAND; WALES

Eccentric detective Sherlock Holmes has been a prolific public figure since his debut in Arthur Conan Doyle's 1887 novel *A Study in Scarlet*. In fact, he holds the Guinness World Record for the most portrayed human literary character in TV and film. While a number of adaptations (both good and bad) have brought him to life, it was the 2010–2017 TV series, *Sherlock*—with Benedict Cumberbatch in the title role and Martin Freeman as his sidekick John Watson—that gave us a fresh take on the brilliant sleuth.

Creators Steven Moffat and Mark Gatiss came up with the detective series while working as writers on *Doctor Who (p180)*. During long train rides from London to Cardiff (where production for *Doctor Who* was primarily based), they discussed their desire to update Sherlock Holmes, infusing his story with today's modern technology. Their idea keenly resonated with TV executives

187 North Gower Street, a suitable stand-in for 221B Baker Street

Speedy's Sandwich Bar
North London's Speedy's Sandwich Bar & Café was seen throughout the series.

1 Speedy's Sandwich Bar
2 187 North Gower St.

187 North Gower St.
A suitable stand-in for the off-limits Baker Street, this became the detective's home.

3 St. Barts Hospital

4 Aldwych Station

5 Southbank Skatepark

St. Barts Hospital
Season 2 ends on (and off) the roof of St. Barts Hospital in the City area of London.

Battersea Power Station
Watson visits Battersea Power Station, pre-redevelopment, in seasons 2's opening episode.

Southbank Skatepark
Clues are hidden amid the graffiti in this skatepark during season 1, episode 2.

6 Battersea Power Station

Aldwych Station
Holmes and Watson explore the tracks of this abandoned station in season 3's first episode.

FINSBURY · HOXTON · CLERKENWELL · SHOREDITCH · BLOOMSBURY · COVENT GARDEN · SOHO · CITY · SWATER · LONDON · Hyde Park · Kensington Gardens · River Thames · SOUTHWARK · BERMONDSEY · St James's Park · KNIGHTSBRIDGE · WESTMINSTER · PIMLICO · LAMBETH · Battersea Park

and production began in January 2009, with many interior scenes filmed at studios around Wales—convenient for Moffat, who in 2010 became *Doctor Who*'s showrunner, tying him to the country even more.

While Moffat and Gatiss were happy to film much of the series in studios (convenience aside, budgetary reasons were also a factor), they had no interest in moving Sherlock Holmes and his crime-solving exploits out of central London. Consequently, many exterior shots took place around the historic capital. Filming at 221B Baker Street (Sherlock's home in the Conan Doyle books) was a no-go however, with the popular Sherlock Holmes Museum located at the address (in reality, the museum sits between 237 and 241 Baker Street but was given special permission to bear the 221B address). Instead, the show's production turned

the quieter 187 North Gower Street into Sherlock's base. The restaurant just below this address, Speedy's Sandwich Bar & Café, appeared frequently in the series and has since become a landmark for *Sherlock* fans. Other filming locations, including both local establishments and famous sites, are scattered all around the capital—and luckily, you don't need to be a Sherlock-level sleuth to find them.

The London Eye looming over the Thames River, as seen in *Sherlock*'s opening credits

FINDING SHERLOCK

Benedict Cumberbatch might have clinched the lead in *Sherlock*, but other great actors auditioned for the role. Martin Freeman, who became Sherlock's right-hand man Watson, and Matt Smith, who Moffat later cast as the Doctor, didn't make the cut.

THE GRAND BUDAPEST HOTEL

Filmed in and around the town of Görlitz, *The Grand Budapest Hotel* is often considered the high point of Wes Anderson's stylized oeuvre. Visit today and you'll find the scenic German locale still has the movie's whimsical magic.

① Dresden

Dresden's darkly imposing palatial complex, The Zwinger, is where Deputy Vilmos Kovacs flees from the menacing hit man Jopling.

Also in Dresden is the historic Dresdner Molkerei Gebrüder Pfund milk shop. This was the interior of Mendl's pâtisserie.

② Görlitz

Disused department store Görlitzer Warenhaus plays the interior of the hotel. It's currently in the throes of redevelopment.

Various streets around Görlitz also feature in the movie, including Fischmarkt Street and the Brüderstrasse.

④ Karlovy Vary

The Grandhotel Pupp and Hotel Imperial, in this Czech spa town, were said to be the inspiration for the Grand Budapest.

③ Basteibrücke

Beady-eyed fans will recognize this bridge from Agatha and Zero's snowy wedding at the end of the movie.

YEAR
2014

LOCATION
GERMANY

Pretty Fischmarkt Street, in Görlitz, which Agatha cycles along

There's no denying it—Wes Anderson has style. Think of the director's film repertoire and it's not just the romping storylines or quirky characters that come to mind but the unique aesthetic of his movies. Picture-perfect backdrops, pastel-colored buildings, symmetrical façades—these are the fingerprints of the American filmmaker, and they're all over *The Grand Budapest Hotel*.

Following the adventures of hotel concierge Gustave H. and his faithful lobby boy Zero, *The Grand Budapest Hotel* largely takes place in the namesake hotel, located in the fictional village of Nebelsbad, Zubrowka. In order to create this fantastical setting, Anderson searched high and low for an eastern European town with an aristocratic-style hotel. After scouring Budapest, Vienna, and the quaint Czech Republic spa town of Karlovy Vary, he eventually settled on the German town of Görlitz. If Anderson's aesthetic sensibility feels like it's from a bygone era, then he and Görlitz were a match made in heaven. The spa town had emerged from both World Wars in shockingly good nick and its charming buildings had barely aged in centuries. It's this anachronistic feel that makes Görlitz a popular shooting site for period films, including the World War II-set *Inglourious Basterds* (2009) and *The Book Thief* (2013).

Among Görlitz's historical buildings, Anderson found an empty department store, the Görlitzer Warenhaus. With its Art Nouveau framework, stained-glass

Görlitzer Warenhaus, the department store
used for the hotel interior

The building transformed, as featured
in this scene from the movie

ceiling, stately chandeliers, and marble surfaces, the store captivated Anderson immediately. Soon after, it became a hive of film production as the team set about turning its interior into the Grand Budapest. Sets were built in the atrium, evoking the 1930s and 1960s time periods portrayed in the movie. The top floor of the building, meanwhile, was converted into a production office for the crew. Fans are currently unable to venture inside the store, but plans for redevelopment are in the works, so it might not be long before you can run up the staircases and wander along the balcony corridors where the movie's action took place. A short walk from the warehouse is the pink Hotel Börse, where the crew and cast stayed during production. Fun fact: the hotel's owner and staff played extras in some of the movie's scenes.

As fairy tale–like as Görlitz was, the little town didn't have everything. Other scenes took place around Germany, with Dresden chosen as a secondary base for filming. Operating since 1892, the Dresdner Molkerei Gebrüder Pfund milk shop became the interior of the revered Mendl's pâtisserie, where baker Agatha works. Decorated in an ornate, neo-

Renaissance style, featuring hand-painted tiles, the shop is as flamboyant as Agatha's beautiful Courtesan au Chocolat cakes (which sadly aren't available). Also in Dresden is the movie's Kunstmuseum, which Deputy Vilmos Kovacs enters while trying to escape the clutches of Jopling and his terrifying knuckle-dusters. In reality, this is the

A MODEL HOTEL

The Grand Budapest's exterior isn't a Görlitz location; in fact, it's not a real location at all. Several hotels (such as the beautiful Grandhotel Pupp and Hotel Imperial in Karlovy Vary) influenced Anderson's wedding-cake design, which was then brought to life using a selection of carefully crafted miniature models.

Zwinger, a stunning palatial complex and one of the most famous baroque buildings in Germany. A short train ride links Görlitz and Dresden, meaning fans can tour Anderson's whimsical world in one easy trip.

Dresdner Molkerei Gebrüder Pfund milk shop, the perfect setting for the renowned Mendl's

THE REAL WES ANDERSON WORLD

The backdrops of Anderson's fanciful movies don't always look particularly real, but luckily for fans, many of them are.

THE ROYAL TENENBAUMS
(2001)

This comedy-drama about a dysfunctional family was filmed around New York City (the family home is in Harlem), but it was set in a fictionalized version of the city. Consequently, the team avoided showing any key landmarks on screen.

MOONRISE KINGDOM
(2012)

Set on the imaginary island of New Penzance, this coming-of-age tale follows boy scout Sam Shakusky and his pen-pal Suzy Bishop on a whirlwind romance. The film was shot in Rhode Island; Conanicut Island Lighthouse was the Bishops' home.

THE FRENCH DISPATCH
(2021)

Perhaps the most Wes Anderson movie the director has ever made, the *French Dispatch* was shot in the French city of Angoulême. The animated segments were created by local artists in a nod to the city's comic book heritage.

THE ITALIAN JOB

With a career-defining turn by legendary actor Michael Caine, this endlessly parodied 1969 crime romp remains one of the most-loved British movies of all time—and there were as many escapades off screen as there were on it.

YEAR
1969

LOCATION
TURIN, ITALY

A cheeky, charismatic cockney. A car chase featuring Mini Coopers. Ask anyone and they'll probably tell you *The Italian Job* is one of the most quintessentially British movies ever made. Of course, this has little to do with the geography of the movie: the antiquated scenes depicting 1960s London make up just a small part of the adventure. No, the spirit of 1960s Britain was carried by our criminal protagonists right across Europe, with an audacious heist centerpiece, filmed around the streets and rooftop racecourses of Turin in Italy, cementing the movie's place in the nation's heart.

Like the Mini Coopers driven with abandon, the production team had a wild ride in Turin. When staging the traffic jams that would facilitate the gold thieves' escape, the team shut off whole areas of the city, causing real traffic to pile up and infuriating local motorists in the process. Rumor has it that this was done with the blessing, and even the assistance, of the local Italian Mafia.

Turin's Fiat factory rooftop

The Minis in motion, after racing around the Fiat factory

Risky business was a common theme throughout shooting. The unbelievable stunt at the Fiat factory was dangerous enough to pose a legal risk for Michael Deeley, the movie's producer. He later claimed that, in the event of an accident on set, he had arranged a car to drive him to the airport, where a plane was ready to fly him out of the country. Similarly, the Palavela driving sequence was allegedly shot without the permission of Italian authorities, who feared the roof would collapse. The museum manager found out they had started filming and was far from happy, prompting director Peter Collinson to hide until filming wrapped.

And was it all worth it? Of course it was. No matter how many times the movie's heist scene is imitated, there's simply no denying the power of the original. For Michael Caine, the iconic catchphrase must have grown old, but *The Italian Job*—and its 1960s British spirit—is still more than able to blow the bloody doors off.

MINI MAYHEM

Troy Kennedy Martin, *The Italian Job* screenwriter, settled on Mini Coopers for the chase sequence because they were an icon of the 1960s, and a British brand through and through. These nifty, colorful and conspicuously modern vehicles provided a unique contrast to Turin's historic streets.

① **Palazzo Madama**
The gang hurtle down Palazzo Madama's early 18th-century stairs in their trusty Mini Coopers.

②

Galleria Subalpina
The Minis continue their escape through this busy, light-filled arcade.

③ **Palazzo Carignano**
The stolen gold is loaded into the cars in the atrium of this grand palace.

④ **Diga Michelotti**
The cars make it across the Po River using the Diga Michelotti weir.

⑤

Chiesa Parrocchiale della Gran Madre di Dio
The high jinks continue as the cars interrupt a wedding at this church.

⑥ **Torino Palavela**
Our plucky trio take a daring drive up the sail-shaped roof of the Torino Palavela.

⑦ **La Pista 500**
The Minis race around the Fiat factory's test track, which has since been transformed into Europe's largest rooftop garden.

TURIN

Palazzo Madama ①
Galleria Subalpina ②
Palazzo Carignano ③
Diga Michelotti ④
Chiesa Parrocchiale della Gran Madre di Dio ⑤
⑦ La Pista 500
3 km (2 miles)
⑥ Torino Palavela
4.5 km (3 miles)

PIAZZA CASTELLO
PIAZZA CARLO ALBERTO
PIAZZA SAN CARLO
PIAZZA CARLO EMANUELE II
PIAZZALE VALDO FUSI
PIAZZA CARLO FELICE
PIAZZA CAVOUR
PIAZZA MARIA TERESA
PIAZZA VITTORIO VENETO

VIA GIUSEPPE GARIBALDI
VIA SAN FRANCESCO D'ASSISI
VIA PO
VIA GIUSEPPE VERDI
VIA PRINCIPE AMEDEO
VIA PO
CORSO SAN MAURIZIO
VIA GIUSEPPE LUIGI LAGRANGE
VIA ROMA
VIA CARLO ALBERTO
VIA XX SETTEMBRE
VIA SAN MASSIMO
VIA GIOVANNI GIOLITTI
River Po
CORSO CASALE
CORSO MONCALIERI
CORSO CAIROLI
VIA VILLA DELLA REGINA

HOW TO STEAL A MILLION

While high-stake heists are often shot in the studio, they're set in some of the finest galleries, museums, and casinos. Precision planning and catlike stealth is required for these capers, or the alarm is sure to sound.

METROPOLITAN MUSEUM OF ART, US

A New York stalwart, "the Met" was the site of successful heists in both *The Thomas Crown Affair* (1999) and *Ocean's 8* (2018). Only *Ocean's 8* obtained permission to film on site, recreating the famous Met Gala in cooperation with the museum. Forced to film at night, the crew had to construct and deconstruct the elaborate sets each day for the two-and-a-half-week shoot.

TOWER OF LONDON, UK

Whether it's Ricky Gervais in *Muppets Most Wanted* (2014), or the animated *Minions* (2015), all sorts have attempted to steal the Crown jewels from this Beefeater-guarded fortress. Here's a tip: to secure a successful heist, check first that Johnny English is on guard duty. His hilarious incompetence saw the Crown jewels stolen from under his nose in *Johnny English* (2003).

THE LOUVRE, FRANCE

This Parisian gallery is probably best known to fans of the mystery thriller series *Lupin* (2021–), where Omar Sy's protagonist attempts a daring theft of a Marie Antoinette necklace in the opening episode. Surprisingly, few movies have depicted a theft involving the world's most famous painting, the *Mona Lisa*, one being the German movie *The Theft of the Mona Lisa* (1931).

BELLAGIO CASINO AND HOTEL, US

Though a casino card caper may seem the obvious choice at this opulent Las Vegas hotel, George Clooney and co. took a more direct approach in *Ocean's 11* (2001), making off with around $160 million directly from the Bellagio's vault. The cast and crew were able to stay and film on the site with unlimited access due to a producer's friendship with the hotel's owner.

NATIONAL GALLERY, UK

Home to over 2,000 world-class paintings, it's little surprise that London's National Gallery has starred in several heists—both in film and real life. Unruly schoolgirls made off with *Girl with the Pearl Earring* in *St. Trinians* (2007), while Jim Broadbent took on the role of Kempton Bunton in *The Duke* (2020), a retelling of the 1961 theft of the *Portrait of the Duke of Wellington* by a British pensioner.

1 The American Wing courtyard at the Met

2 The Crown jewels, attractive to all manner of thieves

3 Classical sculptures at the Louvre

4 The lit-up Bellagio with its dancing fountains

5 World-class art on display at the National Gallery

1

2

3

4

5

Fort Point ①

Fort Point National Historic Site sits beneath the southern end of the Golden Gate Bridge. It's here that Madeleine unexpectedly jumps into the water.

Fort Point ① San Francisco · Berkeley · Oakland · Manteca

Hayward · Modesto

San Mateo · Fremont

Half Moon Bay · Palo Alto

Sunnyvale · San Jose

Big Basin Redwoods State Park ②

A besotted Scottie and Madeleine walk around Muir Woods, in reality this park, and stop to look at the cross section of an old tree.

Big Basin Redwoods State Park ②

CALIFORNIA

Gilroy

Santa Cruz

Watsonville · Mission San Juan Bautista ③ · Hollister

Salinas

Mission San Juan Bautista ③

This is the mission where Scottie frantically chases Madeleine, before her (supposed) fall from the tower.

Cypress Point ④ · Monterey

④

VERTIGO

San Francisco's beautiful winding streets and dramatic coastal terrain provided the perfect location for Alfred Hitchcock's tale of a man lost in a psychological maze.

YEAR
1958

LOCATION
CALIFORNIA, US

Cypress Point

Scottie and Madeleine share a kiss along this windswept coastal area. The cypress tree in shot was a prop.

Few movies are as suited to their locations as Alfred Hitchcock's *Vertigo* is to San Francisco. The misty Californian city was the ideal backdrop for this film noir, with famously lengthy driving sequences showcasing a range of streets and notable landmarks.

Given the city's starring role, there was one big problem: the director hated filming on location, preferring the controlled environment of the studio instead. Consequently, external scenes—around San Francisco (including at Golden Gate Bridge) and at Big Basin Redwoods State Park and Cypress Point—were shot in 16 days. If possible, Hitchcock stuck to the studio. Even the scenes set in Ernie's, a now-closed local restaurant, were recreated on a set, with the staff hired to act as waiters.

The mission that Scottie drives first Madeleine (an imposter) and then a reluctant Judy to is very real, however. The Spanish Mission San Juan Bautista, dating from the late 1700s, was well used, though a matte shot (a painting on glass placed in front of the camera) replaced the mission's ornate bell tower, which had been destroyed by a recent fire. As for those memorable scenes depicting Scottie's vertigo, for which the director performed his "dolly zoom" technique—they were all filmed back in the studio, of course.

NORTH BY NORTHWEST

Carved onto the face of the sacred Lakota Sioux mountain Six Grandfathers, the looming Mount Rushmore monument is the backdrop for one of cinema's most famous finales.

DID YOU KNOW?

GEORGE R. ROMERO
Romero (p109) was a camera assistant for the scenes at Grand Central Terminal.

HITCHCOCK
The director delayed production so that James Stewart, who expected to play the lead, was busy and Cary Grant (who he wanted) was free.

YEAR
1959

LOCATION
SOUTH DAKOTA, US

You may be surprised to learn that Alfred Hitchcock's *North By Northwest* (widely regarded as one of cinema history's best) was almost called *The Man Who Sneezed in Lincoln's Nose*. Though that catchy title didn't stick, the idea that inspired the movie did. Hitchcock longed to make an espionage thriller where the lead hides from villains in Abe Lincoln's nose (in Mount Rushmore). Though he never makes it into Lincoln's nostril, Cary Grant's ad exec Roger Thornhill does escape from spies, clambering across the faces of the giant American memorial. Well, sort of. Hitchcock was actually refused access to shoot on the monument (due to the movie's violent content), so his team had to get creative. Combining wide shots of the mountain and the national park with practical sets of the renowned sculptures, the crew managed to perfectly recreate the scene the director had envisioned.

Before this famous finale, *North by Northwest* goes on a location-hopping tour, visiting Chicago, New York, and California as part of Roger Thornhill's mistaken identity-fueled adventures. Once these location-based scenes had been shot, the filmmakers headed back to Los Angeles to shoot interiors. While those sets are long gone, movie lovers can still visit Mount Rushmore and gaze up at Abe's giant nostril—just as Hitchcock would've wanted.

Presidential profiles carved into granite at Mount Rushmore

IN BRUGES

Suicidal hit men and Belgium in the bitter winter don't sound like the ingredients for a delightful time, but in the hands of writer/ director Martin McDonagh, *In Bruges* is tragi-comedy at its best.

The Rozenhoedkaai, passed by Ken and Ray on their tour

YEAR
2008

LOCATION
BRUGES, BELGIUM

When Brendan Gleeson and Colin Farrell's odd couple arrive in Bruges, they have more on their mind than admiring the Flemish architecture. Lying low from a mission gone wrong, the pair wander the streets, passing the beautiful buildings and icy blue canals of this charming medieval city.

Martin McDonagh first encountered Bruges on an ill-fated romantic weekend away. Rather than be disheartened by his relationship, he spent his time exploring the city and was struck by its cinematic potential. Bruges is known as "the Venice of the North," and perhaps not so coincidentally the Venice-set movie *Don't Look Now (p124)* was one of the director's inspirations for *In Bruges*.

When he returned to make *In Bruges*, his characters actually stay in the same hotel he did and visit many of the popular tourist sights. (Though you'd assume the violent chase scenes didn't mirror McDonagh's time in the city.) The city's council were more than happy for McDonagh to film in Bruges, too, with most tourist areas allowing production. Only one church would not allow production inside, the Basilica of the Holy Blood, so the Jerusalem Church stepped in to play the role. The council even kept the Christmas decorations up (despite filming taking place in March), to help the director set the scenes.

Bruges quickly becomes a purgatory for the characters and a place where their lives are constantly at risk. While stakes like that mean the movie is hardly feel-good festive fare, *In Bruges* is technically a Christmas movie. Soft carols, twinkly lights, and hit men in hiding—happy holidays from Belgium.

Grote Markt

This beautiful square at the base of the Belfry of Bruges is seen throughout the movie. With its open-air bars and restaurants, it's a popular draw for tourists.

Belfry of Bruges

Tragedy unfolds at this medieval bell tower—the views across the city are wonderful, but it's a long way down to the square below.

Relais Bourgondisch Cruyce

The pair stay in this quaint hotel while stuck in Bruges.

Rozenhoedkaai

When walking into the center, Ken and Ray pass the Rozenhoedkaai quay, one of the best views in the city.

Gruuthusemuseum

Ken and Ray befriend the cast and crew of a movie being shot in the courtyard of the Gruuthusemuseum.

Sint-Janshospitaal

During a forced sightseeing boat trip, Ken and Ray pass the Saint John's Hospital, which dates to the 11th century.

① Grote Markt
② Belfry of Bruges
③ Relais Bourgondisch Cruyce
④ Rozenhoedkaai
⑤ Gruuthusemuseum
⑥ Sint-Janshospitaal

EIERMARKT
PHILIPSTOCKSTR
HOOGSTRAAT
MUNTPLEIN
MOERSTRAAT
BURG
Groenerei
VISMARKT
NOORDZANDSTR.
SIMON STEVIN PLEIN
BRUGES
EEKHOUTSTR
Koningin Astridpark
SCHAARSTRAAT
Coupure
ZUIDZANDSTR.
MARIASTRAAT
NIEUWE GENTWEG
KATELIJNESTR.

6

THE FINAL FRONTIER

As decades of universe-hopping science-fiction movies have shown, the beauty of our planet is that it can pass for anywhere. So otherworldly are some corners of Earth, that a brief trip can take us to our favorite sci-fi locations—*Star Wars*' sands of Tatooine, perhaps, or the icy wastelands of Mann's planet in *Interstellar*—all without ever having to set foot in the Doctor's TARDIS. Earth is sufficiently abundant to have become the number one intergalactic travel destination.

While the use of the green screen has been a boon for the genre—augmenting the world around us, facilitating space sequences, or conjuring corners of new worlds out of nothing—the best sci-fi movies remind us that there's no substitute for the real thing. Luckily, venturing to the final frontier needn't mean leaving terra firma at all.

DUNE

"My road leads into the desert," says *Dune*'s protagonist, Paul Atreides.
Director Denis Villeneuve took this statement quite literally, heading deep
into Jordan to bring the harsh, desert planet of Arrakis to the silver screen.

YEAR
2021, 2023

LOCATION
JORDAN; UAE

The title of Frank Herbert's 1965 sci-fi masterpiece says it all. Predominantly set on the arid Arrakis, *Dune* follows the young Paul Atreides and his family as they battle for control of the planet, the source of the powerful psychotropic drug known as "spice." Despite its bounty, make no mistake: Arrakis is an inhospitable place, blanketed with barren deserts and crawling with deadly sandworms.

Finding somewhere to stand in for such a hostile environment proved the first challenge for directors putting the popular novel to film. While David Lynch chose to shoot in Mexico for his 1984 take, Denis Villeneuve pored over numerous locations for his 2021 adaptation. Being a superfan, he was extremely particular about finding the right backdrops: he spent days in a helicopter, flying over deserts to find the perfect locations. Eventually, he decided Jordan's stunning Wadi Rum was the ideal choice (interestingly,

the area's otherworldly Arabic name translates to "the Valley of the Moon"). The desert terrain of Wadi Rum looks eerily identical to the original 1960s illustrations of Arrakis created by the artist John Schoenherr.

Although Wadi Rum was ideal for certain scenes, the area chosen was bereft of one vital feature: dunes. As the movie couldn't possibly be made without these, Villeneuve was forced to find other locations to stand in for the deep desert of Arrakis. Production designer Patrice Vermette—designated dune-hunter—trawled the deserts of Mauritania, Chad, and Libya on Google Earth, finally selecting the Liwa Desert Dunes in Abu Dhabi for scenes in which Paul, Duke Leto, and Gurney first encounter a sandworm.

For the 2023 follow-up movie, *Dune: Part II,* Villeneuve and his crew would return to the sweeping deserts of the UAE and Jordan—as would the terrifying sandworms.

Wadi Rum *(left)* and the Liwa Desert Dunes *(right)*, the settings for Arrakis

PROMETHEUS

Iceland's ancient appearance—a canvas of hulking glaciers and active volcanoes—easily masquerades as a prehistoric planet in this sci-fi feature.

YEAR
2012

LOCATION
ICELAND

Ridley Scott's return to space saw the director abandon the retro-futurist grime of *Alien* for the wilds of nature instead. His original idea for sci-fi horror *Prometheus* was to shoot in Morocco. However, these plans were scuppered by the Arab Spring uprisings of 2010 and filming was forced to relocate to Iceland.

Fortunately, the move worked out, with the country's primeval landscape perfectly suited to the movie's creationist themes. Throughout *Prometheus*—which follows an astronaut crew into space to discover humanity's extraterrestrial ancestors (the so-called "Engineers")—Scott showcases Iceland's spectacular scenery. Fans first see it in the movie's opening scene, which sweeps across the craterous landscape before settling on the incredible Dettifoss waterfall; this isolated sight perfectly represented Scott's image of the beginning of time. Scenes of the alien planet were also shot around Iceland's Hekla volcano, an unearthly terrain Scott referred to as a volcanic cinder, on account of its distinctive black soil and lava pinnacles.

It's easy to see why NASA sent two astronaut training missions here in the 1960s and why Hollywood returns to this country again and again for space-set movies. Touch down in the middle of a glacier in Iceland and you could easily believe you've left Earth entirely.

INTERSTELLAR

The key to bringing science-fiction blockbuster *Interstellar* to life was not found in the stars but rooted in the wild plains of Canada and the chilly reaches of Iceland.

YEAR
2014

LOCATION
CANADA; ICELAND

Svínafellsjökull glacier or Dr. Mann's ice planet

Digital trickery isn't Christopher Nolan's thing. Wherever possible, the director uses practical effects, grounding his movies in the real world (despite his back catalogue featuring superheroes and metaphysical ideas). In 2017's *Dunkirk*, he shot at the historic site of the evacuation, while in 2023's *Oppenheimer*, he set off real explosives to recreate the nuclear bomb tests. *Interstellar* was no different, with Nolan largely foregoing CGI to give this epic its realistic edge.

While ex-NASA pilot Cooper spends most of the movie searching space for a new home for humanity, *Interstellar* begins on Earth. Here viewers are first introduced to Cooper's farm, a site Nolan's production crew built from scratch (including the cornfields) on a rolling plain in Pekisko, Alberta.

To create the planets Cooper visits, Nolan flew to Iceland, which provided fittingly formidable landscapes. For the scenes on Miller's aqua planet, the crew worked in knee-deep water for days on end. (Anne Hathaway nearly developed hypothermia when a faulty zipper filled her suit with icy water.) Meanwhile, at the Svínafellsjökull glacier, high wind speeds regularly forced the crew to retreat inside and pause filming the scenes on Dr. Mann's ice planet. Despite these imperfect conditions, the realism Iceland's magnificent scenery provided was more than worth the chill.

STAR TREK

While *Star Trek*'s characters boldly ventured into space, the team behind this sci-fi saga stuck largely to Los Angeles studios, with frequent forays into the nearby landscapes of California.

YEAR
1966–

LOCATION
CALIFORNIA, US

A pop culture phenomenon, *Star Trek* is now one of the highest-grossing media franchises of all time. Yet despite its emphasis on interplanetary travel, the franchise had very humble, not to mention terrestrial, origins. When it was first pitched to NBC in 1964, the show was offered a relatively tiny budget, meaning the original series had to make do with filming in Los Angeles studios. In fact, up until the Canada-based *Discovery* (2017) and *Strange New Worlds* (2022), every live-action *Star Trek* series and motion picture was shot in and around the City of Angels, utilizing California's spectacular landscapes.

Of all the locations used around Los Angeles, one in particular was revisited time and time again: Vasquez Rocks. These dynamic, angular rock faces *(p164)*, which jut diagonally across the horizon, are located about 30 miles (50 km) north of the city in the Sierra Pelona Mountains. The franchise first made use of the site in "Shore Leave," an episode in the very first season of *Star Trek: The Original Series* (1966–9), and returned again for "Arena," shooting a memorable fight sequence between Captain Kirk and the lizardlike Gorn on and around the rocks. After multiple otherworldly appearances, in both TV series and movies (including *The Voyage Home, Star Trek,* and *Star Trek Into Darkness*), the spectacular rocks finally appeared as themselves, not as a stand-in, in *Star Trek: Picard* (2020).

Rivaling Vasquez Rocks for the title of most-used location is the vast Griffith Park in the Los Feliz neighborhood of

The Vasquez Rocks, used often throughout the *Star Trek* franchise

El Capitan

In *Star Trek V: The Final Frontier*, Kirk (William Shatner, an avid climber) free-climbs El Capitan. The scene was actually shot on a smaller replica cliff built next to the mountain.

Sunstone Winery

Picard retires to this gorgeous winery, built in the style of a French villa, in his namesake *Picard* series.

CALIFORNIA

Pacific Ocean

El Mirage Dry Lake

This dry landscape became the planet Lambda Paz in the "Final Mission" episode of *The Next Generation*.

Vasquez Rocks

The Vasquez Rocks, near the town of Agua Dulce, remain the most iconic *Star Trek* location.

Los Angeles, a go-to spot for Hollywood movie and TV crews. The pilot episodes of both *The Next Generation* (1987–94) and *Voyager* (1995–2001) were filmed here, introducing viewers to such characters as Captain Janeway, Data, Tom Paris, and William Riker. The park's Bronson Canyon, also known as Bronson Caves, made innumerable appearances (and look out for them in the 1966–1967 *Batman* series), while leafy Fern Dell and Griffith Observatory popped up too.

Pushing (just) beyond the frontiers of Los Angeles, the production team filmed at a number of unmistakable California landmarks throughout the franchise, particularly in San Francisco, where Starfleet Headquarters is based in the shows and movies. In *The Voyage Home* (1986) director Leonard Nimoy shot a huge chunk of the movie around the city, including sequences on the Golden Gate Bridge (which has, to date, featured 36 times in the franchise), in Golden Gate Park, and at the Monterey Bay Aquarium, where Spock (Leonard Nimoy himself) swims alongside two humpback whales.

Venturing farther into the Golden State, the beautiful Sunstone Winery

in Santa Barbara appears as Jean-Luc Picard's château in La Barre, eastern France in all three seasons of his eponymous show. Director Hanelle Culpepper had wanted to shoot these sequences on location in France, but practical reasons kept production for *Picard* local—just as they did for the scrappy original series that started it all. Ironically for a sci-fi franchise with entire planets to explore, a single state was sufficient for a galaxy's worth of incredible locations.

Los Angeles

Griffith Park's Bronson Canyon appeared in numerous *Star Trek* shows and movies—from *The Original Series* to *Star Trek VI: The Undiscovered Country*.

The beautiful gardens of the Tillman Water Reclamation Plant are featured in multiple episodes of *The Next Generation* and *Deep Space Nine*.

California's Sunstone Winery, an ideal retreat for retired admiral Jean-Luc Picard

WESTWORLD (2016–2022) ▶
Vasquez Rocks went back
to its western roots in the first
season of *Westworld*. It was
the setting of a town that
Dolores and William visit on
their travels.

THE MUPPET MOVIE (1979)
In the first Muppet movie,
all-around bad guy Doc Hopper
meets Snake Walker, a sinister
professional frog killer hired
to dispose of Kermit, in front
of the rocks.

VASQUEZ ROCKS

Jutting dramatically out of a barren landscape, these ancient rocks have been a regular guest star on *Star Trek*. But that's by no means the end of their talents.

This jagged desert fortress, found just north of Los Angeles, has stood in for alien planets in the *Star Trek (p162)* franchise on countless occasions. Yet the otherworldly formations—the result of tens of millions of years of seismic revolt—started their silver screen career in westerns. Many wild west movies were shot here, including *Hearts of the West* (1975) and *Blazing Saddles* (1974). The setting was apt: the rocks are named for Tiburcio Vasquez, a 19th-century outlaw who used them as a hideout; their rugged forms provide the perfect cover and vantage point for a gunfight, after all.

Back on that other wild frontier (aka space), the sandstone formations weren't just a stomping ground for the likes of Kirk and co. They also provided a backdrop for other sci-fi classics, among them *Bill and Ted's Bogus Journey* (1991) and *Planet of the Apes* (2001). It's fair to say, then, that Vasquez Rocks have both lived long and prospered.

BUFFY THE VAMPIRE SLAYER
(1997–2003) ▶
During "Restless," the final episode of season 4, Buffy confronts the First Slayer here during an action-packed dream scene.

BILL AND TED'S BOGUS JOURNEY (1991)
The rocks were the setting for Bill and Ted's encounter with Death. The hooded figure tries (and comically fails) to bring them with him to the afterlife.

STAR WARS

A long time ago, George Lucas used real-life locations to transport us to a galaxy far, far away. Now, numerous movies and TV shows later, *Star Wars* still looks to planet Earth for inspiration.

YEAR
1977-

LOCATION
WORLDWIDE

As soon as viewers saw C-3PO and R2-D2 escape Princess Leia's starship and crash-land on the desert world of Tatooine, it was clear that cinema would never be the same again. Since this iconic opening of the original *Star Wars* (since retitled *A New Hope*), director George Lucas's space opera franchise has become a global phenomenon, spawning video games, TV series, theme park rides, and thousands of quirky collectibles.

And it all began on Tatooine, a fictional planet with twin suns and many alien inhabitants. While this new world felt a long way from home, Lucas ensured that Tatooine was believable by filming in real places in Tunisia and ensuring that his characters—for all their talk of hokey religions and ancient weapons—were relatable. This was a sci-fi world that felt lived in, a universe that owed as much to classic Westerns as the future technology of *Star Trek (p162)*.

It might be hard to imagine, given the runaway success of the franchise today, that the cast and crew had little hope that the first movie would be a success. Within a couple of days, production in Tunisia was massively behind schedule, with the region's biggest rainstorm in half a century turning the arid desert (intended to portray Tatooine) to mud. Later, creating any usable visual effects for the space-set scenes became a time-sapping nightmare. Considering these headaches (and others) Lucas and the team encountered, it's amazing the movie made it into theaters at all.

When it did, *A New Hope* (1977) became the highest-grossing movie of the 1970s, and a sequel was inevitable. As the sci-fi adventures of Lucas's beloved characters (Luke Skywalker, Princess Leia, and Han Solo) continued in *The Empire Strikes Back* (1980), the scope of the *Star Wars* universe expanded. Giving each planet its own visual identity was crucial to the creator's world building. Yoda's planet Dagobah was known for its

The setting of Luke Skywalker's boyhood home *(right)* and the still-standing Tatooine movie set *(left)*, both in Tunisia

swamps while the largely uninhabitable world of Bespin was a gas giant. Both these planets, as well as others, were realized on sound stages, but in order to create the ice world of Hoth, the team once again ventured out on location, this time to the snowy reaches of Norway.

Unfortunately, the sought-after setting soon became a hindrance: Norway's coldest winter in 100 years wreaked havoc on production. The team were briefly stranded in the mountain village of Finse and some of their planned locations became inaccessible—several scenes ended up being shot outside the Finse 1222 Hotel where the crew were staying. With such bad luck, Lucas would have been forgiven if he'd never taken *Star Wars* on location again. Nonetheless, trilogy closer *Return of the Jedi* (1983) went back to Tatooine, only this time California's Death Valley became the desert planet and the state's forest of Cheatham Grove the woody Endor.

When Lucas returned to the *Star Wars* galaxy, for the eagerly anticipated prequel trilogy, bigger changes were in store. State-of-the-art set dressing and stunning matte paintings were regularly used to enhance real-life locations used in the original trilogy, but by the 1990s, CGI technology was fast becoming an important tool for Hollywood creatives. In 1997, Special Edition rereleases of Lucas's original trilogy gave the movies a computer-generated makeover, most notably by making the streets of Tatooine a little more lively. By the time the first prequel, *The Phantom Menace*, debuted in 1999, whole worlds were being constructed entirely from pixels.

Salar de Uyuni, Bolivia's unearthly salt flats, as seen in *The Last Jedi*

ICELAND
Reynisfjara **5**
Hardangerjøkulen **6**
NORWAY FINLAND
SWEDEN
Derwentwater
DENMARK
IRELAND U.K. GERMANY
POLAND
Skellig Michael **8** **9** Puzzlewood
FRANCE
Villa del Balbianello **10**
ROMANIA
ITALY **11** Dubrovnik
SPAIN Palace of **12**
Caserta TURKEY
Plaza de España **13** GREECE
TUNISIA
Tozeur **14** **15** Hotel Sidi Idriss
MOROCCO IRAQ IRAN
16 Wadi Rum
ALGERIA LIBYA EGYPT SAUDI AFGHANISTAN
ARABIA PAKISTAN
MAURITANIA **17** Rub' al Khali
OMAN INDIA
MALI NIGER CHAD SUDAN YEMEN
SENEGAL
GUINEA NIGERIA ETHIOPIA SRI
CÔTE LANKA
D'IVOIRE CAMEROON KENYA Laamu Atoll **18**
GABON DEM. REP.
OF THE CONGO
TANZANIA

RUSSIA KAZAKHSTAN UZBEKISTAN KYRGYZSTAN TURKMENISTAN CHINA

Indian
Ocean

Atlantic
Ocean

ANGOLA ZAMBIA
NAMIBIA ZIMBABWE MADAGASCAR
BOTSWANA
SOUTH
AFRICA

1 Cheatham Grove
This giant redwood forest was used to film the speeder bike scenes on the Forest Moon of Endor in *Return of the Jedi*.

2 Death Valley
After running out of time and money during *A New Hope*'s Tunisia shoot, the team filmed scenes with the Jawa sandcrawler here.

3 Tikal Temple
After seeing this Mayan temple on a travel poster, George Lucas sent a unit to Guatemala to film the location for the Rebel base in *A New Hope*.

4 Salar de Uyuni
The world's largest salt flat (a bleached-white expanse in Bolivia) is where the

Resistance held off the First Order's offensive on Crait in *The Last Jedi*.

5 Reynisfjara
Rogue One (2016) begins with a shuttle arriving on this black Icelandic beach (the planet Lah'mu).

6 Hardangerjøkulen
The ice planet Hoth was filmed on this Norwegian glacier in *The Empire Strikes Back*.

7 Derwentwater
This is the location of the battle between Resistance X-Wings and First Order TIE Fighters in *The Force Awakens*.

8

Skellig Michael
Luke Skywalker seeks refuge from his past on the rugged isle of Ahch-To, or Skellig Michael, in *The Force Awakens* and also in *The Last Jedi*.

9 Puzzlewood
This leafy forest in Gloucestershire was a location for Takodana, the home of Maz Kanata's castle of outlaws.

10 Villa del Balbianello
Padmé and Anakin escape to this CGI-enhanced Lake Como villa in *Attack of the Clones* (2002).

11 Dubrovnik
The streets of this ancient Croatian city make an appearance as Canto Bight, a gambling city on the planet of Cantonica in *The Last Jedi*.

12 Palace of Caserta
Formerly home to Italian royalty, this grand palace appears in *The Phantom Menace* and *Attack of the Clones* as the Theed Royal Palace on Naboo.

13

Plaza de España
In *Attack of the Clones* Padmé and Anakin walk around this plaza in Seville. The area stood in for the city of Theed on the planet Naboo.

14 Tozeur
The movie set for the city of Mos Espa, the Tatooine home of Anakin Skywalker, is still standing near Tozeur, Tunisia. Nearby is the Chott el Djerid salt lake, where the igloo-shaped home of Luke Skywalker was left after filming *A New Hope*.

15

HOTEL SIDI IDRISS
STAR WARS

Hotel Sidi Idriss
This hotel, in the Tunisian town of Matmata, was the interior of Luke's boyhood home in *A New Hope*.

16 Wadi Rum
Jordan's Wadi Rum played the planet Pasaana in *The Rise of Skywalker* (2019) and the moon Jedha in *Rogue One*.

17 Rub' al Khali
The planet of Jakku, in *The Force Awakens*, was shot in this desert in the UAE.

18 Laamu Atoll
These islands in the Maldives were used as the planet Scarif in *Rogue One*.

Puzzlewood, where Rey encounters Ren in *The Force Awakens*

But for all the creative freedom CGI provided, the three prequels arguably struggled to capture the tactile magic of their predecessors. After Disney's multi-billion-dollar buyout of Lucasfilm in 2012, it was no surprise when director J. J. Abrams chose to take the saga's comeback movie *The Force Awakens* (2015) out on location. As well as adding another desert planet to the galaxy (the scenes in Jakku were shot in Abu Dhabi), the movie's production team shot numerous scenes in Ireland and the UK,

SPOT THE CELEB

The *Star Wars* sequel trilogy isn't short of great cameos. Daniel Craig plays a stormtrooper and Simon Pegg is Unkar Plutt in *The Force Awakens*. Meanwhile, Tom Hardy, Prince William, and Prince Harry all reportedly played stormtroopers in deleted scenes for *The Last Jedi*.

paying visits to the Lake District's scenic Derwentwater, Gloucestershire's mossy Puzzlewood, and Greenham Common's retired RAF base. *The Force Awakens* also introduced viewers to Luke Skywalker's island sanctuary: the Irish isle of Skellig Michael proved as stunning a backdrop as anything ever created on a computer. Fun fact: during filming on this same

island in *The Last Jedi* (2017), the resident puffins had a habit of getting in the shot; instead of digitally removing the birds, the team ended up replacing them with computer-generated porgs instead.

As Disney+ has shifted *Star Wars'* priorities toward TV, another evolution has taken place. *The Mandalorian* (2019–), *The Book of Boba Fett* (2021–2), and *Obi-Wan Kenobi* (2022) have all been filmed using StageCraft, a vast digital backdrop of LED screens that surround the actor on set. These huge walls can feature footage filmed on location, meaning actors can interact with a "real place," so to speak. The technology is becoming increasingly popular as an alternative to green screens (where background footage is added during postproduction, not during live filming). As Jon Favreau, the creator of *The Mandalorian*, put it: "the location is [now] brought to the actors."

While traveling to a galaxy far, far away may be off the table (for now), setting foot anywhere that helped bring Lucas's saga to life is a dream for fans. Just catching a glimpse of Tunisia's deserts or the isle of Skellig Michael is enough to get John Williams's famous theme tune playing in your head.

Ireland's craggy Skellig Michael, the isolated home of Luke Skywalker in *The Force Awakens*

TUNISIA ON THE BIG SCREEN

The original location for Tatooine, Tunisia went on to become one of Hollywood's favorite filming spots.

MONTY PYTHON'S LIFE OF BRIAN
(1979)

When naughty boy Brian Cohen famously tells the Romans to go home, he's actually in Tunisia. A number of locations here—including the Ribat in Monastir—filled in for the Holy Land.

RAIDERS OF THE LOST ARK
(1981)

Producer George Lucas returned to Tunisia with Harrison Ford for Indiana Jones's first big-screen adventure *(p86)*. The movie's Egypt scenes were mostly shot around Kairouan, including the moment when Indy shoots a show-boating swordsman.

THE ENGLISH PATIENT
(1996)

Based on Michael Ondaatje's novel, Anthony Minghella's Academy Award magnet made extensive use of Tunisian locations. The cities of Tunis, Mahdia, and Sfax all masqueraded as 1930s Cairo in the movie.

CLOSE ENCOUNTERS OF THE THIRD KIND

When Steven Spielberg's benevolent aliens touched down at Wyoming's Devils Tower, the otherworldly rock became a cinematic landmark. But this distinctive formation already had an epic mythology before the aliens turned up.

YEAR
1977

LOCATION
WYOMING, US

Following the stresses of shooting *Jaws (p112)* in the waters off Martha's Vineyard, director Steven Spielberg insisted that his follow-up, *Close Encounters*, would be filmed on sound stages, without any location shoots. However, the scale of this space-age story meant that Spielberg soon backtracked (much to his later regret, with the over-budget movie described by the director as "twice as bad and twice as expensive" as *Jaws*).

The majority of *Close Encounters* was shot in Mobile, Alabama, where two airship hangers, part of Brookley Field Industrial Complex, housed the movie's enormous sets. Out in the natural world, Devils Tower, a huge igneous rock standing 1,267 ft (385 m) above the Wyoming landscape, took on a now iconic starring role. This unique rock tower became the first national monument in the US in 1906 (you can thank the person who left the apostrophe out of that very proclamation for the grammatical error in its name). The site is sacred to several Indigenous groups,

all of whom have different oral histories about it. For the Cheyenne people, it's known as Bear's House or Bear's Lodge and the rock's markings were created by a bear's claws. Located far from any major human population, the tower is free from signs of light pollution. It's this ethereal quality that gave Spielberg the impetus to transform the rock into a huge intergalactic antenna, not only attracting alien visitors, but humans (including Richard Dreyfuss's Roy Neary) drawn toward an encounter beyond their wildest dreams.

Model of Devils Tower created by UFO-obsessed Roy Neary in his living room

The colossal Devils Tower, natural wonder and landing spot for the alien mothership

South Grand Island Bridge

Abandoned cars block this striking bridge, which spans the Niagara River, in *A Quiet Place: Part II*.

Akron

This charming village featured as the Abbott's home town in the opening of *A Quiet Place: Part II*.

Wallkill Valley Rail Trail

The alien attack at the start of *A Quiet Place* was shot at the Springtown Bridge, on the scenic Wallkill Valley Rail Trail.

Little Falls

Main Street in Herkimer County's Little Falls was closed for two days to portray an abandoned town during the filming of the first movie.

Lee takes son Marcus to shout in safety at Buttermilk Falls, just to the north of Little Falls.

A QUIET PLACE

All is quiet in this tense back-to-basics sci-fi horror, with the movie's low-key, upstate New York locations ensuring every alien encounter feels shockingly real.

YEAR
2018, 2020

LOCATION
NEW YORK, US

When the human race is decimated by aliens who use their acute hearing to hunt, any sound can be the difference between life and death. But look past the movie's ingenious "don't make a noise" premise (eating popcorn in the theater has rarely felt so awkward) and *A Quiet Place* is simply the story of a family battling to survive.

Indeed, the fact that everything feels so relatable is one of the main reasons for the movie's success. Director John Krasinski opted to shoot at real-life locations in upstate New York, turning the area's leafy forests and local towns into hunting grounds for the sharp-of-ear alien invaders. Isolation is the best hope of survival, so the Abbott family turn a remote farmhouse (in Pawling, New York) into a protective fortress. The movie's climactic scenes take place here, making full use of the surrounding cornfields—which didn't exist before the area was chosen. The production team bought 20 tons (20,000 kg) of corn and hired local farmers to grow it to a height just tall enough to hide an alien.

A Quiet Place was such a huge success that a sequel inevitably followed, letting the monstrous aliens loose in New York state all over again.

PREDATOR AND PREY

Locating its hunting grounds in the sweltering jungles of Mexico and the icy rivers of Canada, the *Predator* franchise always puts its cast through its paces.

YEAR
1987, 2022

LOCATION
MEXICO; CANADA

Since its release in 1987, *Predator* has carved out a legacy as one of the most intense alien-horror franchises of all time. That reputation has more than a little to do with the first movie's legendarily tough shoot in the steamy jungles of Mismaloya (not far from the resort of Puerto Vallarta) and the waterfalls near Palenque (including the stunning Misol-Ha), both in Mexico.

Predator's roster of Hollywood actors needed to be believable as special forces soldiers (and capable of taking on an alien predator), so military adviser Gary Goldman was hired to put them to the test. Agonizing runs through the jungle (which was crawling with red ants and coral snakes) and weapons training in the heat followed, and once filming started, it only got harder. A brutal workout regime was spearheaded by Arnold Schwarzenegger (Major Dutch in the movie) who led the cast on daily morning workouts in a gym he had imported and built in a hotel ballroom.

Over three decades and four movies later, the franchise would relocate to the US's Northern Great Plains for a more stripped-back story, but a no less physical shoot. Amber Midthunder trained for four weeks to prepare for her lead role in *Prey*, which would see her swimming in glacial rivers and wielding tomahawks. Most of the movie was shot in the Stoney Nakoda Nation, showcasing the incredible scenery of Alberta, Canada, and providing a rare look at Comanche life in the 1700s. In the midst of it all? The intergalactic hunter that's *nearly* impossible to kill.

Mismaloya's jungle, the hunting ground of the Predator

DID YOU KNOW?

MUST GO FASTER

When escaping the attacking aliens, Jeff Goldblum repeats this famous line, which he previously uttered in *Jurassic Park (p94)*, in a nod to director Steven Spielberg.

ENOLA GAY

The B-29 bomber famed for dropping the world's first atomic bomb was once based at Wendover Air Base.

K-Y JELLY

The alien invaders were coated in K-Y Jelly to give them their slimy appearance. It had to be regularly applied as the heat caused the substance to evaporate within minutes.

INDEPENDENCE DAY

Arriving on Earth with all of that attitude, *Independence Day*'s technologically advanced extraterrestrials failed to anticipate the antics of a plucky US marine in this seminal sci-fi blockbuster.

YEAR
1996, 2016

LOCATION
UTAH, US

The arid salt flats, across which Will Smith's character drags his alien prisoner

Much of *Independence Day*'s run time is spent reveling in the destruction of some of the US's most famous buildings, yet scenes shot on a little-known natural landmark proved just as memorable. An endless sheet of blinding white, the dazzling Bonneville Salt Flats stretch across northwest Utah's vast desert. The flats are the ideal stand-in for any alien landscape but in *Independence Day*, they remained very much on Earth.

We first encounter the Bonneville Salt Flats when Captain Stephen Hiller drags his alien captive to the nearby El Toro Air Base. It's a scene that stands out in memory, not only for the remarkable landscape but for Will Smith's comic turn as Hiller. After trash-talking his unconscious prisoner, Smith blurts out the unscripted line: "And what the hell is that smell?" During winter, the flats are covered in a thin film of water, in which untold millions of brine shrimp lay their eggs, ready to hatch come spring. When they die and decompose in just as large numbers, they produce a putrid smell—one strong enough to force a Hollywood star to ad-lib his disgust on camera.

Director Roland Emmerich returned to the area for the climactic battle in the sequel *Independence Day: Resurgence*, though a recent windstorm left the salt

Wendover Airport, seen as both El Toro Air Base and Area 51 in the movie

flats compromised by dirt, and rather beige as a result. Luckily, the spectacle of a 220 ft (67 m) tall alien chasing a school bus provided ample distraction from the off-white hue.

Nearby Wendover Airport (which was an Air Force Base until 1965) doubled as El Toro Air Base and Area 51, where President Whitmore gives his rousing speech to humanity from the back of an armored truck. At one point in the movie's production, the US military was on hand to help with props, vehicles, and locations, but they quickly withdrew their support when the studio refused to remove all the references to Area 51 from the script. For conspiracy theorists, that's a move quite as whiffy as the Bonneville Salt Flats themselves.

ALIENS ATTACK!

When it comes to extraterrestrial invasion, some cities (and their most visited tourist haunts) don't tend to fare well. Should little green men appear, it's best to give these places a wide berth.

LOS ANGELES, US

As well as earthquakes, infections, and even a sharknado, Los Angeles has been subject to alien attacks. Its on-screen destruction began with *The War of the Worlds* in 1953 (miniatures and puppetry were used for the invasion) and continued with *Battle Los Angeles* (2011). The latter was, in fact, filmed in Louisiana, where the production team built a huge replica of LA in Baton Rouge.

THE WHITE HOUSE, US

The White House has been attacked on film more times than Meryl Streep has been nominated for an Oscar, and the culprits are often extraterrestrial. Since being targeted in the classic 1956 alien invasion flick *Earth vs. The Flying Saucers*, it's been destroyed by Martians in *Mars Attacks!* (1996) and then blown to smithereens by a City Destroyer spacecraft in *Independence Day (p176)*.

MOUNT RUSHMORE, US

In both *Superman II* (1980) and *Mars Attacks!*, off-world invaders deface this US sight, replacing the presidents' features with marks of their own. Of course, the monument didn't get any face-lifts in real life; instead, tiny scale models were used.

NEW YORK CITY, US

"They like to get the landmarks," declares Jeff Goldblum's character in *Independence Day: Resurgence (p176)*. He's right, especially when it comes to New York. The Empire State Building is lasered into oblivion by aliens in the original *Independence Day*. The city is also home to the alien-busting team's headquarters in *Men in Black* (1997), with eccentric behavior encountered on its streets explained away as being typically extraterrestrial.

LONDON, UK

A (now-demolished) council estate in London's Elephant and Castle sees plenty of action in *Attack the Block* (2011), when a group of listless teens are forced to battle furry aliens with glowing teeth. This wasn't the first or last time London was set upon by creatures from another planet; places like Canary Wharf and Westminster have been attacked by *Doctor Who (p180)* baddies, including the Daleks, while Greenwich was the site of a battle finale in *Thor: The Dark World* (2013).

1 Looking out over LA before the aliens arrive

2 The White House being destroyed in *Independence Day*

3 Mount Rushmore's sculptures, often defaced by aliens

4 The Statue of Liberty, a landmark for the taking

5 The now-demolished Heygate Estate, invaded by aliens in *Attack the Block*

1

2

3

4

5

DOCTOR WHO

Despite having all of time and space at their fingertips, the Doctor can often be found on our home planet, with the ever-evolving Time Lord frequently saving the day in spots across the UK.

The Tower of London, the unexpected home of UNIT command from 1999 onward

YEAR
1963–

LOCATION
ENGLAND; WALES

Since *Doctor Who*'s 1963 debut, the Doctor and their faithful TARDIS have traveled through time and space—and into the hearts of fans along the way. Running for over half a century, this BBC show has never been afraid of embracing change, as shown by the regular renewal of its lead Time Lord. Yet one thing remains steadfast throughout the decades of adventures and grandiose speeches: filming nearly always takes place in the UK, regardless of whichever planet or era the Doctor has traveled to.

During its initial run, *Doctor Who* was frequently filmed at the BBC-owned (and now-defunct) Lime Grove Studios in London, with occasional forays to surrounding streets. The UK capital's eclectic mix of architecture, along with narrow alleyways and iconic landmarks, was ripe for alien showdowns. The second season episode "The Dalek Invasion of Earth" saw Daleks scattered across the city's most famous sights, while "The Web of Fear" episode from season 5 involved furry Yetis strolling through the tunnels of a London Underground station. Permission to film in the tunnels was refused so a set was built that was so realistic, London Transport threatend to sue the BBC.

❷

Westminster Bridge
"The Dalek Invasion of Earth," with William Hartnell as the Doctor, saw Daleks dotted along this bridge.

❸

Theed St.
The "Remembrance of the Daleks" episode, starring Sylvester McCoy as the Doctor, was filmed on this historic street.

❹

Clink St.
The Tom Baker-era "The Talons of Weng-Chiang" was shot along this street near Borough Market.

❺

Tower of London
The heavily walled Tower of London has been the home of UNIT command during the revival series.

❶

❻

The Shard
Matt Smith's Doctor pauses on St. Thomas Street before driving his motorcycle up the side of The Shard in "The Bells of Saint John."

Brandon Estate
The Brandon Estate in Southwark was home to Rose Tyler in the revival series.

WHITECHAPEL

CITY

COVENT
GARDEN

SOHO

River Thames

Tower of
London **❺**

Clink St. **❹**

Theed St. **❸**

❻ The Shard

SOUTHWARK

Westminster **❷**
Bridge

LONDON

LAMBETH

WALWORTH

KENNINGTON

VAUXHALL

Brandon **❶**
Estate

Burgess
Park

Battersea
Park

PRODUCTIONS SHOT AT BAD WOLF BAY

Southerndown Strand's scenic shores have been more than just a parallel Earth beach.

MERLIN
(2008–2012)

This fantasy drama, starring Colin Morgan as the titular character, showcased this beach's natural beauty in "The Labyrinth of Gedref," an episode in its very first season.

SHERLOCK
(2010–2017)

Largely shot in Wales, this series *(p142)* made its way to Southerndown Strand in its fourth and final season for "The Final Problem"; the beach is seen as helicopters arrive at Sherrinford high-security prison.

HEARTS OF FIRE
(1987)

A movie starring Bob Dylan, *Hearts of Fire* details the drama between a rock star and his young protégé. It didn't win critics' hearts, but it did showcase the beach in all its glory.

Doctor Who faced cancellation in 1989, but—just like the Doctor regenerates to circumvent death—the show was revived in 2005. This time around, London wasn't the center of the Time Lord's universe. The BBC expanded production of its varied programs to other UK regions in the 2000s, with *Doctor Who*'s new showrunner, Russell T. Davies, moving all of time and space to Cardiff. The success of "Nu-Who" provided funds for a permanent production base: Roath Lock Studios, where corridors were specifically built to allow two Daleks to comfortably pass through side by side.

With Cardiff the new home of *Doctor Who* (and spin-off series *Torchwood*), the city became a go-to for location shots. Roald Dahl Plass's open space became a TARDIS refueling station, while the plaza's Water Tower, a shimmering 70 ft (21 m) tall structure, became known as "Torchwood Tower" after the spin-off's titular alien-hunting organization's headquarters were based here.

Farther afield, Cardiff's picturesque surrounding landscapes stood in for various settings. Rolling green hills dotted with cottages became historical English villages and lush green forests transformed into alien worlds. Most famously, the beach of Southerndown Strand became Bad Wolf Bay; it's here that the Doctor and Rose Tyler bid their teary farewells.

While the stunning scenery of Wales provided the perfect outdoor settings,

the country also offered plenty of castles for historical episodes. Built in the 11th century, Cardiff Castle has become a frequent filming location. You'll spot it in the season 6 two-parter "The Rebel Flesh" and "The Almost People," with its dim hallways overrun with "fleshy fluid" doppelgangers. The castle's ornate library also appears as the TARDIS library in "Journey to the Centre of the Tardis" (season 7), when viewers see a TARDIS room other than the console or a corridor for the first time.

With filming set to continue in Wales for the next series (which, as of 2023, sees production shift from Roath Lock to a new home at Bad Wolf Studios), the list of locations in and around Cardiff will undoubtedly grow. Fortunately, with distances in the UK so short, you won't need a TARDIS to visit them.

Southerndown Strand, where Rose and the Doctor bid farewell

1 ↖ **National Botanic Garden of Wales**
40 km (25 miles)

Pontypridd

Cwmbran

Ebbw River

Caerphilly

Caerphilly Castle **5**

Newport

M4

Caldicot

Tredegar House **6**

Llantrisant

Thornhill

Pyle

Pencoed

M4

Bridgend

Llandaff City **4**

River Taff

M4

Pentwyn

Penylan

Porthcawl

WALES

Ely

☐ *See Cardiff
inset map, below*

Bristol Channel

Portishead

ENGLAND

M5

**Southerndown
Strand** **2**

Cowbridge

Dyffryn Gardens **3**

7 **Roald Dahl Plass**

Penarth

Llantwit Major

Barry

CARDIFF

PARK PLACE

NORTH ROAD

Bute
Park

BLVD DE NANTES

8 **National
Museum Cardiff**

NEWPORT RD

**Cardiff
Castle**

QUEEN STREET

9

CASTLE ST

10 **Queens Arcade**

River Taff

HIGH ST

THE HAYES

ADAM ST

**① National Botanic
Garden of Wales**
This huge botanical
garden played the
Hydroponics Centre in
David Tennant's "The
Waters of Mars."

**② Southerndown
Strand**
This rock pool–strewn
coastal area has a special
place in the Whoniverse
for its memorable part as
Bad Wolf Bay.

③ Dyffryn Gardens
These botanical gardens
became the grounds of
Versailles in "The Girl in
the Fireplace."

④ Llandaff City
Amy Pond's home village
of Leadworth in "The
Eleventh Hour" was
filmed in Llandaff City,
another show regular.

⑤ Caerphilly Castle
This castle becomes a
monastery in "The Rebel
Flesh" and also appears
in "Vampires of Venice."

⑥ Tredegar House
This National Trust
house is another regular
location. You'll see it
in "Tooth and Claw"
and as the inside of
Versailles in "The Girl
in the Fireplace."

⑦ Roald Dahl Plass
The revived series was
filmed in Roath Lock
Studios and frequently
used this nearby plaza
for location shots.

**⑧ National Museum
Cardiff**
Appearing in many
episodes, this museum
most famously played
Paris's Musée d'Orsay in
"Vincent and the Doctor."

⑨ Cardiff Castle
This castle often shows
up in the series, including
in the "The Rebel Flesh"
and "The Almost People"
two-parter.

⑩ Queens Arcade
The first episode of
"Nu-Who" began with
mannequins attacking
Rose Tyler in this
shopping arcade.

7

THE THRILL OF THE CHASE

The mere mention of a classic action movie will no doubt bring to mind a particularly bombastic set piece: special agent Bond pursuing a baddie through the streets of Istanbul, Maximus seeking revenge in Ancient Rome's Colosseum, or Bruce Willis dangling from Nakatomi Plaza. Audiences love a well-executed fight or a good chase, and if the sequence is done right, it hauls us along for the ride, yelling "hasta la vista!" as we dispatch another foe.

But any great action sequence requires a journey, and journeys requires suitable locations. The most memorable achieve a perfect synthesis between character and setting, and in typically audacious action movies, these settings tend to be big: imposing skyscrapers, smoking volcanoes, endless desert dunes, even vast ocean tunnels. Wherever the drama unfolds, the locations are often just as epic as the mayhem taking place.

JAMES BOND

Since it's very first outing, the *James Bond* movie franchise has shot on
location, taking secret agent 007, a lucky production crew, and an ever
enthralled audience to some of the world's most incredible places.

YEAR
1962–

LOCATION
WORLDWIDE

The turquoise waters around Ochos Rios from which Honey Ryder emerges

If ever there was a character who has endured through the ages, it's James Bond. Since the 1960s, this British secret agent has been living fast and loose, fighting villains, romancing women, and delivering a steady stream of too-often quoted catchphrases. Six actors have played the hero over the course of 25 (official) movies, with more in the pipeline. While the success of the character, and the franchise, can be attributed to a reliable playbook (fast cars, smart gadgets, deliciously evil bad guys) and soaring soundtracks, there's something to be said for the globe-trotting antics of our favorite secret agent. Who can forget Bond and Vesper Lynd sailing into the beautiful city of Venice? Or Bond and M driving through the Highlands of Scotland? Or Honey Ryder emerging from the waters in Jamaica?

Author Ian Fleming may not have had a travelogue in mind when he wrote his popular 007 novels, but by whisking his character from one spectacular setting to the next, his ability to create a sense of place was undeniable. In his first book, *Casino Royale* (1953), Bond traveled to France's luxurious casinos; in the second, *Live and Let Die* (1954), it was New York and Jamaica. The tradition continued for 14 more books. When producers Harry Saltzman and Albert "Cubby" Broccoli began turning the bestsellers into movies (starting with 1962's *Dr. No*), they made sure the locations lived up to the written word.

Most of Fleming's *Dr. No* takes place in Jamaica, which, throughout the series, was something of a second home to Bond (and Fleming, too: he wrote all the Bond books at his home, Goldeneye, on the island, which is now open to guests). Production stayed true to the text, shooting on location. That iconic scene with Ursula Andress was shot at Laughing Waters Beach in Ocho Rios, while others took place in and around the capital of Kingston. The series would return to the country twice more, for Roger Moore's first outing *Live and Let Die* (1973) and Daniel Craig's swan song *No Time to Die* (2021); for Bond fans, a trip to Jamaica is surely top of the list.

BOND'S CREATOR

The brains behind Bond was no stranger to secret agents. Before he became a well-known writer, Ian Fleming worked for Britain's Naval Intelligence Division, overseeing two intelligence units during World War II. He drew on much of this experience when writing Bond.

As much as Fleming and Bond adored Jamaica, seemingly unlimited travel expenses (and movie budgets) mean Bond is always tailing villains around the world. Some of the most memorable adventures have taken the superspy to Asia, with the crew filming on location in such places as Shanghai, Tokyo, and Thailand's islands. *The Man With the Golden Gun* (1974) introduced audiences to Khao Phing Kan, a gravity-defying natural formation in Thailand's Phang Nga Bay. This stunning landmark is now often referred to as "James Bond Island" due to its starring role, despite actually playing the den of the titular man with the golden gun, Scaramanga (a devilishly devious performance by Christopher Lee).

And it's nearly always the villains who have homes—or should we say lairs?—in remarkable locations. In *You Only Live Twice* (1967), the criminal organization SPECTRE and cat-loving fan favorite Blofeld set up a base in the crater of Japan's Shinmoedake volcano, on the island of Kyushu. Of course, the production team could hardly hollow out the inside of a huge volcano, so the interior of Blofeld's lair was instead built at Pinewood Studios in the UK, a go-to studio for the *Bond* franchise. Production designer Ken Adam's set was of impressive proportions—it was 200 ft (60 m) wide and 55 ft (16 m) high overall—and cost a staggering $1 million to build.

Bond finds himself on the hunt for Blofeld again in *On Her Majesty's Secret Service* (1969). This time around, the action takes place in the Swiss Alps, with Blofeld having secured another

① Golden Gate Bridge
Roger Moore's Bond and ex-KGB villain Max Zorin battle at the top of this bridge in *A View to a Kill* (1985).

② Las Vegas
Diamonds Are Forever (1971) was filmed around Las Vegas, but much has changed since the 1970s.

③ Mexico City
Bond navigates Day of the Dead celebrations in Zócalo (the main plaza in Mexico City) during the opening scenes from *Spectre* (2015).

Just outside the city is Centro Ceremonial Otomí (a site for Otomí cultural celebrations). It's here that

Thailand's scenic Khao Phing Kan, or "James Bond Island"

See Europe map, p191

FINLAND

RUSSIA

UKRAINE

KAZAKHSTAN

MOROCCO

11 **Istanbul**
TURKEY

AFGHANISTAN

CHINA

JAPAN

ALGERIA LIBYA

10 **Gara Medouar**

IRAQ IRAN

PAKISTAN

EGYPT SAUDI ARABIA

18 **Himeji Castle**

Hashima **17**
Island

16 **Shinmoedake Volcano**

12 **Udaipur**

MAURITANIA

MALI NIGER

OMAN

CHAD SUDAN YEMEN

INDIA

15 **Hong Kong**

NIGERIA

ETHIOPIA

SRI LANKA

Bangkok **13**

Pacific Ocean

DEM. REP. OF THE CONGO

KENYA

14 **Khao Phing Kan**

Indian Ocean

TANZANIA

INDONESIA

ANGOLA

Atlantic Ocean

NAMIBIA

MADAGASCAR

AUSTRALIA

SOUTH AFRICA

Bangkok
Despite being set in Ho Chi Minh City, the motorbike stunt scenes in 1997's *Tomorrow Never Dies* were shot in Bangkok.

Khao Phing Kan
This limestone karst tower is known around the world as "James Bond Island" thanks to its role as Scaramanga's lair in *The Man with the Golden Gun*.

drug lord Sanchez hides in a fake religious compound at the end of *Licence to Kill* (1989).

4 Fort Knox
The production team managed to film exterior aerial scenes over Fort Knox and neighboring Godman Air Force Base for *Goldfinger*.

5 New Orleans
At the beginning of *Live and Let Die*, one of Bond's colleagues meets his unfortunate demise at a funeral taking place around the junction of New Orleans's Chartres and Dumaine streets.

6 Seven Mile Bridge
Sanchez makes an escape along this bridge in *Licence to Kill*.

7

Bahamas
Much of *Thunderball* (1965) was shot at Nassau, in the Bahamas. The Vulcan

bomber crash-lands here and the model can still be seen at Clifton Wall.

8

Jamaica
One of the most famous beach scenes in cinematic history —diver Honey Ryder emerging from the sea—was shot at Laughing Waters Beach in Ocho Rios.

The island's Green Grotto Caves played Dr. Kananga's (aka Mr Big) underground lair in *Live and Let Die*.

9

Sugarloaf Mountain
A climactic fight sequence takes place in a cable car descending from this mountain in Rio de Janeiro in *Moonraker* (1979).

10 Gara Medouar
Rising from the Saharan sands of Morocco is Gara Medouar, a circular rock formation that became a meteor crater and home to the headquarters of SPECTRE in *Spectre*.

11

Istanbul
The opening of *Skyfall* features a car chase that builds through the streets of Istanbul and speeds through the Grand Bazaar. Bond had been here before in *From Russia with Love* (1963).

12 Udaipur
The Taj Lake Palace in Udaipur was the floating headquarters of Kamal Khan in *Octopussy* (1983)—it's now a hotel. Just outside the city, the historical Sajjangarh Monsoon Palace played his lair.

15 Hong Kong
Bond visits The Peninsula Hong Kong hotel in *The Man with the Golden Gun*.

16 Shinmoedake Volcano
This active volcano in Kirishima National Park was the setting for Blofeld's secret missile base in *You Only Live Twice*. The interior was a set in England.

17 Hashima Island
Japan's Hashima Island is seen during *Skyfall* as the home of the main antagonist Silva. The street scenes, however, were studio sets.

18 Himeji Castle
The ninja camp in *You Only Live Twice* was set in the hilltop Himeji Castle, in Hyōgo. Built from 1333 onward, it's the largest castle in Japan.

DID YOU KNOW?

DOWN UNDER

James Bond has never been to Australia or New Zealand.

CORKSCREW CAR JUMP

The corkscrew car jump from *The Man with the Golden Gun* was the first movie stunt to be calculated by computer.

THE NAME'S BOND

007 is named after ornithologist Dr. James Bond; Ian Fleming came across the name in a bird-watching book.

DANIEL CRAIG

Craig had more serious injuries on set than all the other Bond actors combined.

Atlanterhavsveien, in Norway, a scenic setting for a car chase in *No Time to Die*

scenic hideout at the top of a mountain. Filming, again, took place on location; production part-funded construction of the lair (in reality a restaurant), and Piz Gloria, as it was known in the movie and to this day, is still open for business.

If a villain's lair affords opportunity to showcase somewhere spectacular, so too does another set piece from the franchise: the classic chase sequence. Over the years, Bond has hurtled down ski slopes, sped along scenic roads, and hotfooted it across incredible cities, all in pursuit of someone invariably up to no good. *Goldfinger* (1964) sees Sean Connery wind along Switzerland's extraordinary Furka Pass in his favorite car, the Aston Martin DB5. The same car is taken for a spin in *GoldenEye* (1995) by Pierce Brosnan, for a thrilling chase along the scenic Route de Gentelly in France. Daniel Craig's Bond also has some great drives under his belt.

In *No Time to Die*, he speeds across the Atlanterhavsveien (Atlantic Ocean Road), an incredible road that connects some of Norway's rugged islands. And when he's not behind the wheel? Then you'll find him on a motorcycle instead. *Skyfall*'s (2012) opening sequence sees the secret agent careening through Istanbul's bustling bazaars and racing along rooftops, giving fans a whistle-stop tour of the city as he goes. In *No Time to Die*, he hops on his bike again in Matera, a beautiful old Italian city. For a road trip with a difference, look to the Bond movies for inspiration.

While Bond inevitably spends a huge amount of time racking up air miles, he is, ultimately, a British agent, and London has always been his home. Or is it Scotland? Although his famous employer, the British Secret Service MI6, operates out of London throughout the series—and plenty of scenes are filmed around the capital (speed-boat down the Thames River, anyone?)—

1 Atlanterhavsveien
Bond drives across the stunning Atlantic Ocean Road in Norway during *No Time to Die*.

2 Glen Etive Rd.
This scenic road near Glencoe, Scotland, stretches toward Bond's old home, Skyfall.

Piz Gloria
This revolving restaurant in the Swiss Alps played Blofeld's secret hideout in *On Her Majesty's Secret Service*.

4 Furka Pass
In *Goldfinger,* Bond has to test the cornering of his Aston Martin DB6 on this Swiss road.

5 Verzasca Dam
GoldenEye's opening sees Pierce Brosnan's Bond leap from this massive dam in Switzerland. It's now a popular spot for bungee jumping.

6 Ice Q
Fans can dine at this modern restaurant in Sölden, Austria, which features in one of the main action sequences in *Spectre*.

7 Cortina d'Ampezzo
This Dolomite ski resort was a key location in *For Your Eyes Only* (1981); the ski and bobsled stunts were all filmed locally.

Venice
The city makes repeated appearances in the movies, including during *Moonraker*'s memorable gondola chase scene.

9 Matera
Multiple scenes in *No Time to Die* take place at this Italian city, also seen in *Wonder Woman (p42)*.

10 Capriccioli Beach
Bond's car emerges from the sea here in *The Spy Who Loved Me* (1977).

Bond actually comes from Scotland. Audiences were treated to a glimpse into the agent's past in Daniel Craig hit *Skyfall*. Featuring yet another incredible driving sequence, along the Glen Etive Road near Glencoe, the movie takes us to Bond's family home in the Highlands. Fans making the pilgrimage will have to make do with the Scottish scenery, however—the house doesn't exist in real life and was built on a set in England.

Still, anyone hoping to follow in Bond's footsteps will have more than enough epic locations to fill a lifetime (and a passport). From Mexico to Morocco, Jamaica to Japan, Bond might be the silver screen's most prolific traveler. Ambitious on-location production has grounded the franchise in the beauty of real-world locations, ensuring the sometimes anachronistic agent feels relevant and up-to-date. People may ask, who will play the next Bond? For those with the travel bug, the real question is, where will he travel next?

BLADE RUNNER

The dystopian future (the year being 2019) of Ridley Scott's noir masterpiece *Blade Runner* was brought to life with a mix of models, backlot sets, and real Los Angeles landmarks.

YEAR
1982

LOCATION
CALIFORNIA, US

The shadowy Los Angeles of the (then) future was vital to the look and feel of *Blade Runner*. In this dystopian thriller/noir detective story, Ridley Scott gives us a gritty version of a Los Angeles in a time of outer space colonies and robotics. It's a world both familiar and alien, where flying cars swoop above advertising-lit buildings and hardened former cops (such as Harrison Ford's Rick Deckard) track down runaway replicants (androids).

Turning the famously sun-kissed city into a gloomy cyberpunk nightmare required six months of shooting, all at night. It was a grueling schedule that needed the production team to convert busy venues like the Bradbury Building into futuristic locations over the course of just a few hours. Once filming had wrapped for the night, they had to clean up in time for office workers to arrive at 9 a.m. Oft-used movie locations like the 2nd Street Tunnel were also transformed using smoke and xenon spotlights.

Blade Runner's backdrops weren't all real, though. The city's rain-slick streets were shot on the Warner Bros. Studios backlot, repurposing its artificial "New York Street" section. Miniature models were also used to create some of the movie's more dystopian locations. The opening cityscape and towering Tyrell Corporation pyramid were purpose-built for the movie—miles of fiber-optic lighting cables ran beneath the models to give the impression of a living city emerging from the shadows.

During filming, Ford began to grow disillusioned with Scott, who frequently

LA's Bradbury Building, office by day, movie set by night

❶ Warner Bros. Studios

Nearly all of *Blade Runner*'s street scenes were shot in the studio's "New York Street" area. A rain machine and a plethora of neon signs helped transform it into Scott's image of Los Angeles.

❷ Ennis House

The carport of Frank Lloyd Wright's Ennis House is seen when Rick Deckard returns home. The inside of the apartment was built on a studio set and included fake tiles copied from the house.

Santa Monica Bay

isolated himself in the video viewing booth and refused to agree whether Ford's character was human or android. This friction between them would last for years after the movie's release. Yet the director's vision of a crumbling city overlaid with technology became hugely influential. You could trace the entire cyberpunk genre back to *Blade Runner*, with murky screen cities—from Gotham in *The Dark Knight* trilogy *(p36)* to the *Cyberpunk 2077* video game—all inspired by Scott's vision of Los Angeles.

FIT FOR A MOVIE

The Bradbury Building in downtown Los Angeles, known for its ornate ironwork, sky-lit atrium, and open elevator shafts, has been featured in numerous movies. Aside from its role in *Blade Runner*, it's also appeared in romantic comedy-drama *(500) Days of Summer* (2009) and silent feature *The Artist* (2011).

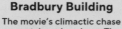

❸ Bradbury Building

The movie's climactic chase scene takes place here. The building's light-filled atrium is a regular location for sci-fi movies thanks to its iron- and brickwork.

❹ 2nd Street Tunnel

Futuristic cars (called "spinners") frequently travel through this tunnel in the movie.

❺ Union Station

The old ticketing hall in Union station was filled with smog and sparsely lit to become Deckard's dystopian police station.

The dazzling lights of LA, which transforms into a dystopian, cyberpunk city in Ridley Scott's *Blade Runner*.

DIE HARD

Action classic *Die Hard* made a leading man out of Bruce Willis and put a once ordinary office building in downtown Los Angeles on the map.

YEAR
1988

LOCATION
CALIFORNIA, US

When studio bosses at 20th Century Fox went looking for a location to shoot *Die Hard,* they didn't stray far from home. After briefly considering an office complex in Houston, Texas, they settled on their new headquarters, Fox Plaza. The building had been recently completed in Century City, Los Angeles (which, appropriately enough, had once been part of the studio's back lot).

Since most of the movie's action takes place in the fictional Nakatomi Plaza, it was vital that the interior of Fox Plaza provided a suitably interesting backdrop for detective John McClane's fight against Hans Gruber and his fellow thieves. Production designer, Jackson De Govia, therefore made full use of the Plaza's air ducts and lift shafts. De Govia later said of the Plaza: "it was meant to be looked at in the same way that a leading man takes over a movie." The majority of filming took place in the building at night, once the lawyers and executives were safe at home, allowing director John McTiernan to run amok, detonating explosions, staging chaotic gunfights and having Willis ride on top of the building's elevators for his role as McClane.

These days, the building attracts both admirers of 1980s "power architecture" and movie fans alike. It's an operating office building, however, so yelling out Willis's legendary (albeit explicit), catch-phrase: "Yippee-ki-yay…" might raise more than a few eyebrows.

Fox Plaza, reassuringly free of Gruber and his group

Plummer St.

When chasing John Connor in *Terminator 2*, the T-1000 drives off a bridge at Plummer St. into the LA River.

Griffith Observatory

The Terminator arrives in 1984 beside movie location favorite, the Griffith Observatory. He then begins his mission: to kill Sarah Connor.

Carrows Restaurant

Sarah Connor works at Big Jeff's diner, which was filmed in the Carrows Restaurant in Pasadena. You can still grab brunch here.

Elysian Park

During a moment's rest in *Terminator 2*, Sarah dreams of witnessing Judgment Day while standing in Elysian Park.

Santa Monica Place Mall

In *Terminator 2*, John meets two Terminators at the same time at the "Galleria"—a scene filmed at this large outdoor shopping mall.

Map labels:
1. Plummer St.
2. Griffith Observatory
3. Carrows Restaurant
4. Elysian Park
5. Santa Monica Place Mall

SIMI VALLEY, SAN FERNANDO, NORTHRIDGE, SUN VALLEY, VAN NUYS, BURBANK, PASADENA, HOLLYWOOD, SANTA MONICA, DOWNTOWN, EL MONTE, COVINA, CULVER CITY, INGLEWOOD, HAWTHORNE, REDONDO BEACH, CARSON, TORRANCE, PALOS VERDES, SAN PEDRO, Santa Monica Bay

TERMINATOR

This science-fiction classic tells of a cyborg's relentless hunt of Sarah Connor, with the streets of Los Angeles bringing James Cameron's series to life.

YEAR
1984, 1991

LOCATION
CALIFORNIA, US

The vision of a metal skeleton clawing its way through the flames came to director James Cameron in a dream, birthing his idea for *The Terminator* (1984). But how could a burgeoning filmmaker afford to shoot an apocalyptic movie about sentient cyborgs? Easy. Cameron scripted a sci-fi slasher set in present-day Los Angeles.

Armed with the guerrilla filmmaking techniques he had learned from former boss Roger Corman, Cameron filmed mostly at night to supplement the movie's gloomy atmosphere. It wasn't just the aesthetics that were on the director's mind, though. Budgetary restraints also forced him to select streets illuminated by mercury-vapor lights, because he didn't have money for electrics.

Production remained thrifty by filming several scenes without permits, too—one, where the Terminator steals a car, was shot in broad daylight by just Cameron and Arnold Schwarzenegger. Sarah Connor's final scene was filmed by a small unit on a desolate California road. The crew fobbed off highway patrol by saying they were shooting a student film.

Cameron returned to the streets of LA to shoot *Terminator 2: Judgment Day* in 1990. Like its predecessor, the sequel was set in the (then) present, with locations like the highway and the mall becoming focal points for bombastic action set pieces. Luckily, most of these places remain untouched, making them ideal pilgrimage spots for fans.

THE LA RIVER

If the LA River looks familiar, that's probably because it is. A long, angular stretch of gray concrete, it has starred in countless movies over the decades, thanks to its urban appearance.

This stretch of sun-baked concrete might not be the first thing that springs to mind when someone says the word "river." Stretching for a total of 48 miles (77 km) from the city's northwest to its south, the LA River was concreted over in 1938 by army engineers as a flood prevention measure. But what it lost in natural brilliance, it made up for with sheer visual impact: it's stark, urban, and industrial, giving it an aesthetic found in few other places on Earth.

It's the perfect place, then, for a zombie to attack in *Fear the Walking Dead* (2015–2023) or for an ambush to take place in *Point Blank* (1967). But where the river really excels is hair-raising scenes: a space shuttle makes an odds-defying landing here in the movie *The Core* (2003), while the shape-shifting T-1000 relentlessly hunts John Connor down its claustrophobic concrete channels in *Terminator 2: Judgment Day (p195)*. After somewhere for your next chase scene? You know where to come.

ALL QUIET ON THE WESTERN FRONT (1930) ▶
In 1930, the flat riverbed was still in its natural state, making it the perfect stand in for no-man's land in this World War I movie.

GREASE (1978)
Near the end of the movie, there's a drag race between Danny and Leo. They zoom along the concreted riverbed between the 1st and 7th Street bridges, cheered on by their friends.

TERMINATOR 2 (1991) ▶

The original Terminator, Arnold Schwarzenegger, powers down the river on a motorcycle, trying to rescue John Connor from the terrifying T-1000, which is chasing him down in a careening truck.

DRIVE (2011)

Providing a contrast to the rest of the nail-biting car chases in this action-packed, neo-noir thriller, the scene where Driver, Ryan Gosling's character, cruises along the river is almost tranquil.

No car chases today: vehicles beneath the BMT West End Line subway

THE FRENCH CONNECTION

William Friedkin's gritty cop drama is celebrated for its breakneck car chase, which was filmed beneath an elevated New York subway track. As it turns out, shooting the scene was just as exhilarating.

YEAR
1971

LOCATION
NEW YORK, US

It was the car chase to end all car chases. With 1971's *The French Connection*, director William Friedkin redrew the boundaries of what cop movies could look, feel, and sound like. It had grit, moral ambiguity, and an ambitious car chase sequence, which saw Gene Hackman's Detective Popeye Doyle drive after a murderer escaping in an elevated subway train.

Surprisingly, the chase was a late addition to the movie, conceived when Friedkin and one of the producers strolled around New York City just one week before filming started. "We watched all of the things that were happening in the city—the smoke coming from the streets, the rumble of the subway beneath our feet—and we sort of spitballed [it]," he later recalled to *Entertainment Weekly*.

The scene itself (shot in Bensonhurst, a residential area of Brooklyn) proved complicated to film—and more than a little dangerous. Friedkin and his team never secured proper filming permits, instead relying on off-duty police officers to flash badges and help corral

6
60th St. and 14th Ave.
The train comes to a crashing halt at 62nd St. station; Popeye is waiting to capture hit man Pierre Nicoli at the bottom of the stairs.

BROOKLYN

KENSINGTON

60th St. and 14th Ave. **6**

BAY RIDGE

New Utrecht Ave. **5**

86th St. and New Utrecht Ave. **4**

NEW YORK CITY

3 86th St.

2 25th Ave. Station

1 Bay 50th St. Station

CONEY ISLAND

5

New Utrecht Ave.
Popeye continues to speed down New Utrecht Ave.; meanwhile, Nicoli the hit man is running out of options on the train.

4
86th St. and New Utrecht Ave.
Popeye swerves to avoid an oncoming woman and her pram at 86th and New Utrecht Ave.

3
86th St.
Popeye continues up 86th St. dodging cars and checking the train above as he drives.

2
25th Ave. Station
Making it to 25th Ave. station before the train arrives, Popeye runs to the platform just in time to see the train fly through without stopping. He gets back in the car.

1
Bay 50th St. Station
At the start of the chase, Popeye fails to commandeer passing cars before finally managing to stop a Pontiac beneath Bay 50th St. He turns the car around to head north onto Stillwell Ave.

Narrowly avoiding mother and child, Popeye's car strikes a pile of trash

traffic. At one point, the director told stunt driver Bill Hickman that he was underwhelmed by the previous day's takes. Eager to impress, Hickman reacted by driving at full throttle through the streets of Brooklyn, with Friedkin filming all the action from the back seat. It's claimed that the car reached speeds of up to 90 mph (145 km/h) at points during its 26-block drive, encountering a few unscripted collisions along the way (but rest assured that Popeye's terrifying near-miss with a woman and her pram was very much staged).

Four years later, Gene Hackman would return to the world of Popeye Doyle for 1975's *The French Connection II*. The movie was a highly successful sequel, relocating its protagonist to Marseille, France, but without that one unforgettable car chase. For fans, the original remains hard to beat.

DID YOU KNOW?

THE CRASH
Halfway through the chase, Popeye crashes into a white car; this was a real accident, with most drivers unaware filming was in progress.

$40,000
Production paid an agent $40,000 to allow filming on New York's trains. Knowing he'd get fired, the agent also requested a one-way ticket to Jamaica.

SATURDAY NIGHT FEVER
John Travolta's dance drama was shot in the streets around 86th and New Utrecht six years after *The French Connection*.

THE MUMMY

Locations as diverse as bustling Marrakesh, the spectacular Sahara Desert and a Kent dockyard formed the backdrop for this rip-roaring adventure.

YEAR
1999

LOCATION
ENGLAND;
MOROCCO

Unlike the 1930s Universal movies (which were never shot outside California) that inspired *The Mummy*, this 1920s-set actioner was a truly global affair. Director Stephen Sommers intended to shoot location scenes in Egypt, but political instability made it impossible, so filming moved to Morocco. Here, Marrakesh doubled as Cairo (the crew spent two weeks taking down telephone lines and TV aerials to make the city look period accurate). To the east of Marrakesh, Gara Medouar—a vast rock formation resembling a meteor crater—became the setting for the lost city of Hamunaptra. The set took around 16 weeks to build and was then completely destroyed as part of the movie's climax.

After a six-week shoot in Morocco—which saw several of the crew airlifted to hospital after being bitten by spiders and scorpions (luckily not flesh-eating scarab beetles)—Sommers headed to the UK. Here, he shot the interiors of the Museum of Antiquities at Mentmore Towers in Buckinghamshire and built a set replicating Giza's port in Kent's Chatham Dockyards—it even featured a working steam train. All in all, the stand-ins worked, and the movie proved highly successful (aided, of course, by the undeniable charm of Brendan Fraser).

GLADIATOR

This sword-and-sandal epic, set during the age of the Roman Empire, crossed continents in search of equally awe-inspiring surroundings.

YEAR
2000

LOCATION
ENGLAND; ITALY; MALTA; MOROCCO

Ridley Scott's tale of Maximus Decimus Meridius had all the trappings of a cinematic epic: gripping Roman source material, a visionary team of actors, writers and producers, and a host of grand locations.

Gladiator begins with a huge battle sequence, shot in Surrey's leafy Bourne Wood *(p44)* in England. If you thought the burning trees looked worryingly realistic, you'd be right. The Forestry Commission planned to cut back part of the forest around the time of filming, but Scott persuaded it to let him burn the trees down for the scene instead.

After this sequence, the action moves through some beautiful landscapes. The home of Maximus's wife and son, ultimately ravaged by Commodus's men, was filmed in the Italian hills of Val d'Orcia, while the scenes where Maximus is forced into gladiatorial combat were shot around the historic town of Aït Benhaddou in Morocco. Maximus then makes it to Ancient Rome, or rather Malta. Here, the team built a 52 ft (16 m) high replica of the Colosseum to film the gladiator scenes.

It's *Gladiator*'s strong sense of place that marks it as a movie worthy of cinema's golden age, with its legions of loyal fans still very much entertained.

The rolling hills of Val d'Orcia, the setting for Maximus's home

KILL BILL

Quentin Tarantino's two-part revenge thriller sent its katana-wielding protagonist all over, from Texas to Tokyo. Yet despite its globe-trotting adventures, filming never strayed far from Tarantino's beloved LA.

YEAR
2003, 2004

LOCATION
**CALIFORNIA, US;
JAPAN**

Tarantino the man was born in Knoxville, Tennessee, in 1963. But Tarantino the legend was born in a video rental shop in Los Angeles, the city to which he moved at the age of three. The cultural and cinematic heritage of LA permeates the director's oeuvre, from *Reservoir Dogs* (1992) to *Once Upon a Time … in Hollywood* (2019). And when the story takes him away from LA? Look closely and you'll still see the City of Angels.

Originally conceived by Tarantino and Uma Thurman while filming *Pulp Fiction* (1994), *Kill Bill* follows Thurman's "the Bride" on her quest for revenge against a team of deadly assassins. Across the two movies, she traverses thousands of miles, traveling around the US and even flying to Japan. While Tarantino, too, made his way to Japan, filming scenes along Tokyo's neon-lit Yasukuni-dori street and over the city's colorful Rainbow Bridge, he shot most of the

The 2nd Street Tunnel, used to recreate a Tokyo street scene

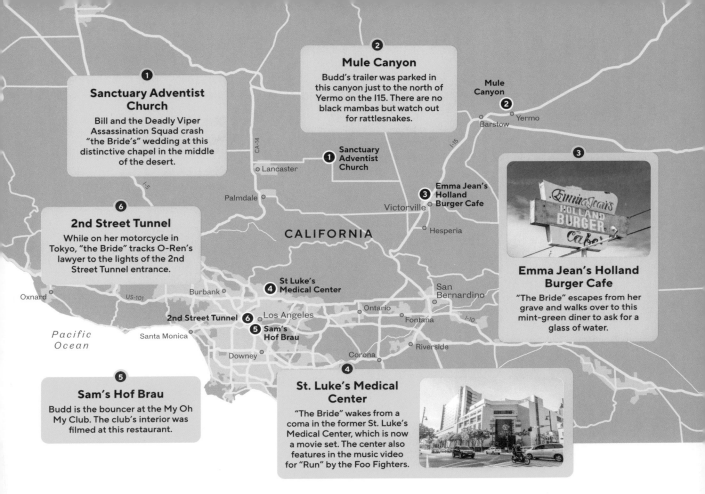

① Sanctuary Adventist Church

Bill and the Deadly Viper Assassination Squad crash "the Bride's" wedding at this distinctive chapel in the middle of the desert.

② Mule Canyon

Budd's trailer was parked in this canyon just to the north of Yermo on the I15. There are no black mambas but watch out for rattlesnakes.

③ Emma Jean's Holland Burger Cafe

"The Bride" escapes from her grave and walks over to this mint-green diner to ask for a glass of water.

⑥ 2nd Street Tunnel

While on her motorcycle in Tokyo, "the Bride" tracks O-Ren's lawyer to the lights of the 2nd Street Tunnel entrance.

⑤ Sam's Hof Brau

Budd is the bouncer at the My Oh My Club. The club's interior was filmed at this restaurant.

④ St. Luke's Medical Center

"The Bride" wakes from a coma in the former St. Luke's Medical Center, which is now a movie set. The center also features in the music video for "Run" by the Foo Fighters.

---

movie in the town he knows best. Local diners, defunct medical centers, and desert backdrops were all utilized, as was LA's 2nd Street Tunnel—which also appeared in 1982's *Blade Runner (p192)*—becoming a roadway in urban Tokyo.

The movie's most recognizable location is the Two Pines Church, an isolated chapel in Texas in which "the Bride" is attacked and left for dead. In reality? It was filmed a two hours' drive from LA, in the middle of the Mojave Desert. Originally built as a community center called The Hi Vista Community Hall, the structure (now the Sanctuary Adventist Church) has long been a resource for filmmakers. It became a chapel in 1981 thriller *True Confessions*, appeared in 1999 actioner *Desert Heat*, and even had

a role in the music video for "Road to Nowhere" by Talking Heads.

"The Bride" may have traveled far and wide to chase down those who dared to wrong her, but for movie buff Tarantino, LA proves hard to shake.

The Sanctuary Adventist Church (or the "Kill Bill church" as it's often known), in California

CROUCHING TIGER, HIDDEN DRAGON

To bring the fantastical *Crouching Tiger, Hidden Dragon* to life, director Ang Lee traveled to some of China's most breathtaking natural locations, and even paid a visit to one of the world's largest movie studios.

YEAR
2000

LOCATION
CHINA

Director Ang Lee's wuxia classic *Crouching Tiger, Hidden Dragon* is packed with perfect fight choreography, incredible acting, and epic cinematography. But adapting the story from Wang Dulu's *Crane-Iron* book series was far from the seamless fantasy Lee and his crew presented. Filmed in China and made for just $15 million (compare that to fellow 2000 release *Gladiator* and its $103 million budget), this wasn't the type of movie Lee could throw money at to fix. The director later commented that filming in China was "pretty impossible," and at times it seemed like finishing his masterpiece might be just that.

So what went wrong? First, action legend Michelle Yeoh injured her knee, needing over a month of rehab in the US. The crew also got lost in the Gobi Desert for an entire day—just as they found their way back, a storm hit. Meanwhile, the flying fight scenes in Anhui's Mukeng Bamboo Forest were incredibly time-consuming to shoot, with the actors precariously suspended on wires.

Yet despite the delays, the rewards were great. With its rolling dunes, vast plains, and unique rocky outcrops, the barren Gobi Desert was a fitting home for outlaw Lo. Similarly, the sea of sky-scraping bamboo trees in Anhui made the fight scene between Li and Jen truly unforgettable.

Filming was undeniably easier when production moved to China's gigantic Hengdian World Studios, in Zhejiang Province, but it's arguably the director's arduous on-location shots that made the movie so memorable.

China's Gobi Desert, where Jen Yu falls in love with outlaw Lo

①

Aberdeen Harbor

At the beginning of the movie, the boat to Han's island (where the martial arts tournament takes place) is seen leaving this area.

Bruce Lee Statue

This statue, on the Avenue of Stars in Tsim Sha Tsui, pays tribute to the martial arts hero.

②

King Yin Lei

The exterior of Han's huge villa was the Cantonese King Yin Lei mansion in the Mid-Levels area. The building is usually open for visitors six weekends a year.

③

Jetty

The stone jetty where Lee arrives on Han's island is beneath the Pacific View development in Stanley. A path to the east of the development leads to the jetty.

④

Cape Collinson Chinese Permanent Cemetery

Lee mourns his mother and sister at this sprawling city cemetery.

ENTER THE DRAGON

Catapulting its hero "Lee" (martial arts master Bruce Lee) to international stardom, this groundbreaking fight movie was shot in locations around Hong Kong.

YEAR
1973

LOCATION
HONG KONG

After years of struggling in Hollywood, an aspiring Bruce Lee returned to his childhood home of Hong Kong, seeking the leading roles America had denied him. Three Hong Kong–set smash hits followed, setting him up for what would become the most influential martial arts movie of all time: *Enter the Dragon*.

Following Lee as he infiltrates a top martial arts tournament on crime-lord Han's private island, the Warner Bros.–backed movie was set and shot around Hong Kong. Costs were a big reason for shooting locally; the movie had a budget of just $850,000 (it grossed more than 400 times this figure).

Not that low budget had to mean low impact. *Enter the Dragon* blasted onto the silver screen, gripping audiences with its grueling fight scenes, all of which were carefully choreographed by Lee. During the dungeon fight, the inimitable warrior swiftly dispatches a then unknown Jackie Chan (who plays an uncredited henchman). Meanwhile, the genre-defining mirror room fight, when Lee defeats Han, was filmed by a cameraman hiding inside a cabinet covered with mirrors; small holes were cut out for the camera to film through.

While *Enter the Dragon* cemented Lee's status as a kung fu legend and worthy star of the big screen, he wasn't around to witness his fame, dying only weeks before the movie's release. Fortunately, this classic ensures his legacy lives on.

THE DA VINCI CODE

Dan Brown's conspiracy thrillers take place in an array of historical landmarks. Yet when it came to adapting the series, controversial plot points meant the movie crew wasn't always welcome in the book's locations.

YEAR
2006

LOCATION
ENGLAND; FRANCE; SCOTLAND

The beauty of Dan Brown's novels is that they act as travel guides in themselves. Focusing on the mystery-fueled ventures of Professor Robert Langdon, the series takes readers from city to city, uncovering historical conspiracies as it goes. The books seem like the perfect fodder for filmmakers, right?

Well, not quite. Many locations in *The Da Vinci Code*, Brown's second book in the series, are religious sites and the plot contains heretical theories, casting aspersions on aspects of the Catholic Church. As a result, several churches closed their doors to production. Take Saint-Sulpice, for example, a prominent church in Paris that is featured heavily in the antics of Langdon (played by Tom Hanks). In the book, the brass groove on its floor is described as belonging to the Paris Meridian (or Rose Line), leading to the mystical "keystone." But this is all fiction; in reality, the brass line in Saint-Sulpice is part of an 18th-century sundial. The church forbade filming inside, and to this day, a notice for tourists debunks the book's premise. The scene was instead shot on a set.

London's Westminster Abbey also boycotted the movie on religious grounds. As a result, the cathedrals in Winchester and Lincoln (both Church of England properties) stood in for the abbey. Both establishments were admonished by a variety of religious communities for getting involved, something Winchester Cathedral answered by using the funds it received from the movie to host an exhibition debunking Brown's book.

Westminster Abbey, where scenes from the movie were set, but not shot

Rosslyn Chapel

The Da Vinci Code's finale takes place in this Scottish chapel. Although filming did take place inside, the exterior was a model (the real chapel was behind scaffolding at the time).

Lincoln Cathedral

This hulking cathedral stood in for Westminster Abbey, after the abbey refused to participate.

Belvoir Castle

This castle was altered with CGI to become the Pope's summer residence, Castel Gandolfo.

Burghley House

Some interior shots of Castel Gandolfo and Chateau de Villette were filmed at this grand house, which also doubled as Windsor Castle in *The Crown* (2016–).

IRELAND

① Rosslyn Chapel

Lincoln Cathedral ②

Belvoir Castle ③

UNITED KINGDOM

④ Burghley House

Westminster Abbey ⑤

Winchester Cathedral ⑥

BELGIUM

GERMANY

LUX

Chateau de Villette ⑦

⑧ Paris

FRANCE

Westminster Abbey

Robert Langdon, Sophie Neveu, and Sir Leigh Teabing visit Sir Isaac Newton's tomb at this monumental abbey; only exterior shots were filmed here.

Winchester Cathedral

One of England's most historic buildings, this cathedral stood in for Westminster Abbey's interior.

Château de Villette

Langdon and Sophie visit the home of Sir Leigh Teabing, played by the Château de Villette to the northwest of Paris.

Paris

The exterior of the church of Saint-Sulpice is featured in the movie; the interior shots were a set.

The site of *The Da Vinci Code*'s first murder and final clue is the Louvre Museum. The authorities gave director Ron Howard rare permission to film here.

DID YOU KNOW?

SISTINE CHAPEL

To help recreate this chapel for the sequel, *Angels and Demons*, the crew posed as tourists and surreptitiously took about 250,000 photos in the Vatican.

RELIGIOUS PROTESTS

Sister Mary Michael prayed outside Lincoln Cathedral for over 12 hours in protest at *The Da Vinci Code* filming on this site.

LINCOLN CATHEDRAL

The bells at Lincoln Cathedral were silenced for the first time since World War II for filming.

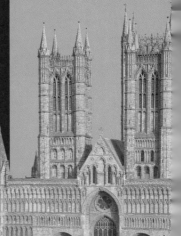

One pivotal landmark that did grant the crew access was the Louvre Museum in Paris. The *Mona Lisa* you see on screen is a replica, though, and the team had to follow various rules while filming at the museum; the script may have asked for blood on the museum floor, but that simply wasn't permitted.

Langdon's engrossing quests through pseudo-history were set in some of Europe's most impressive landmarks. And while Hanks and the crew couldn't enter some of these splendid locations while filming, you certainly can—both Westminster Abbey and the church of Saint-Sulpice are open to visitors.

HOT FUZZ

Edgar Wright's action-comedy saw the tiny Somerset city of Wells transformed into idyllic Sandford, a Gloucestershire village with a strong neighborly community and a dark, murderous secret.

YEAR
2007

LOCATION
WELLS, ENGLAND

Director and writer Edgar Wright grew up in the city of Wells and loved the idea of setting a wild Hollywood action movie in his low-key hometown. *Hot Fuzz* became just that. This hit comedy (the second in the director's *Three Flavours Cornetto* trilogy) sees Simon Pegg's strait-laced Sergeant Nicholas Angel embroiled in a buddy cop adventure that takes the riotous action of American blockbusters to the sleepy streets of an English village.

The director's knowledge and affection for Wells is clear from scene to scene; "I love it but I also want to trash it" he told the *BBC*. Typically ordinary settings have their moment in the sun: the quaint market square, the local supermarket, and the unharmonious village fête all provide the backdrop for brash action sequences, putting another chance of Sanford winning the elite Village of the Year award in serious jeopardy. Famous people also make incongruous cameos in the movie; look out for Cate Blanchet, Peter Jackson, and Wright himself, who poses as a shelf-stacker in the local supermarket—the same job he had in that store before making his feature film, *A Fist Full of Fingers* (1995).

Hot Fuzz doesn't just use Wells as a set, though; it takes full advantage of its historic features. An intricately carved steeple of Somerset stone falls on a local reporter's head and an on-the-run local swan becomes one of Angel's nemeses. The city's beautiful cathedral, however, isn't featured in the movie; Wright digitally removed it to maintain the illusion of a small, local village.

The Crown at Wells pub, a double for Sandford's boozer

Market Place, in Wells, which stood-in for Sandford

But for all that *Hot Fuzz* makes fun of being stuck in Sandford, by the movie's end, there's still the Gothic architecture, Tudor timber ceilings, and pretty gardens to please the eye. It's easy to see why Pegg's once reluctant London cop is unwilling to head back to the big city.

5

City News

Sergeant Angel and partner Danny grab an ice-cream cone from a newsdealer on the main street.

2

St. Cuthbert's Church

The eventful village fête at St. Vincent's Church was filmed on the grounds of the medieval St. Cuthbert's Church.

4

Swan Hotel

The external shots of Sergeant Angel's hotel were taken at this 600-year-old building.

SADLER STREET

4 Swan Hotel

6 Market Place

City News **5**

7

The Crown at Wells

UNION STREET

WELLS

3

Somerfield (Peacocks)

CHAMBERLAIN STREET

PRIEST ROW

1

St. Cuthbert's Church **2**

HIGH STREET

Little Theatre

ST CUTHBERT STREET

Bishop's Palace

Moat

6

Market Place

Appearing throughout the movie, but most notably during the huge shoot-out at the end, is the Market Place.

1

Little Theatre

This venue was the site of an awful production of *Romeo and Juliet* in the movie.

3

Somerfield (Peacocks)

The UK supermarket Somerfield is long gone and the building is now a clothes store. The parking lot remains unchanged.

7

The Crown at Wells

The outside of the village pub was filmed here. The Royal Standard of England, near Beaconsfield, played the interior.

MISSION: IMPOSSIBLE

Spectacular international locations and jaw-dropping stunts are the trademark of the *Mission: Impossible* franchise, which has turned Tom Cruise into a true legend of action film.

YEAR
1996, 2000, 2006, 2011, 2015, 2018, 2023

LOCATION
WORLDWIDE

You've got to hand it to Tom Cruise. Of all the stars who came to fame in the 1980s, he's one of the few not only left standing but who, as he enters his 60s, is still running, flying, and climbing. And thanks to him, the action-packed *Mission: Impossible* series is as fighting fit as ever.

Kick-starting the franchise, director Brian De Palma's *Mission: Impossible* had all the trappings of a spy thriller: double-crossing agents, gadgets galore, and a European city setting, Prague. Though the movie finished with a bang (who can forget the helicopter in the Channel Tunnel), it was John Woo's sequel that upped the action content, establishing the series' globe-trotting credentials along the way. *Mission: Impossible II*'s (2000) opening scene is perhaps one of the most memorable of the series: picture Ethan Hunt as he climbs a canyon face at Dead Horse Point in Utah. It's heart-in-mouth stuff, even more so knowing that Cruise performed the steep climb himself, rejecting Woo's suggestion that they use CGI or climbing doubles. The rest, as they say, is history.

The crew had hit upon something that would define the franchise: a stunning location coupled with a dangerous stunt performed by the plucky star himself. And audiences couldn't get enough.

At points in the franchise, Cruise has hung from the outside of a moving plane, raced a helicopter high over New Zealand's Southern Alps, and held

Tom Cruise climbing a canyon face at Dead Horse Point *(right)* in *Mission Impossible II*

THE THRILL OF THE CHASE

Preikestolen

This towering cliff in Western Norway appeared in the last scenes of *Fallout*.

Volkswagen's Autostadt Wolfsburg

The *Ghost Protocol* team didn't actually film here, but they did recreate the spot in a Canadian hanger.

Prague

As the plan to stop the rogue agent unravels in the first movie, Ethan is seen running across the historic Charles Bridge.

When the team later find themselves under attack, Ethan witnesses a car blown up beneath the bridge, on the picturesque Na Kampě street.

The "embassy" in *Mission: Impossible* was Prague's Národní Muzeum. Internal filming focused on the opulent stairs and main entrance.

Vienna

Ethan escapes from the roof of the Vienna Opera House in *Rogue Nation* (2015).

Burj Khalifa

One of the most renowned images from the series sees Cruise hanging from the exterior of the world's tallest building, the Burj Khalifa, during *Ghost Protocol*.

Royal Palace of Caserta

This royal residence in Caserta, Italy, doubled as the Vatican in *Mission: Impossible III* (2006).

Casablanca

The Hassan II Mosque is seen in the background of a frantic car chase though Casablanca in *Rogue Nation*.

London

At the end of the first movie, Ethan and Luther Stickwell relax with a drink on the balcony of the Anchor Bankside pub.

Ethan meets an old friend in the city's always-busy Liverpool Street station toward the end of the first movie.

Blenheim Palace

Film regular Blenheim Palace appears in *Rogue Nation* as the setting for a black-tie charity ball.

The needle-shaped Burj Khalifa rising above Dubai's many skycrapers

his breath for six and a half minutes in a daring underwater stunt. One of the all-time greatest moments, however, came in 2011's *Mission: Impossible—Ghost Protocol,* when Cruise scaled the 2,722 ft (830 m) exterior of Dubai's Burj Khalifa skyscraper (more than double the height of the Empire State Building). The hair-raising stunt was filmed on the exterior of the tower with views of the city below; 27 windows needed to be removed in order to capture the scene (one of these windows is carried off by Simon Pegg's Benji Dunn).

Before taking on the terrifying climb, Cruise rehearsed for weeks on a 60 ft (18 m) model tower, battling with his body harness, which was so tight it was cutting off his circulation (although it was more secure than Ethan's fictional climbing gloves), and glass that, in the blazing sun, became hot enough to burn his skin. Thanks to his perseverance,

Cruise performed the eight-and-a-half-minute sequence up the Burj Khalifa without a hitch, at one point "falling" 40 ft (12 m). Stunt coordinator Gregg Smrz nervously joked that, should Cruise really fall, the drop was long enough for the actor to send a final text on his way down.

Cruise even found time to take a quick photograph of himself perched casually atop the tower, which, much to the delight of the studio's publicity department, went viral instantly. "This has never been done before, and it'll never be done again because they're never going to allow it," said Smrz. While Cruise has endeavored to top the thrilling sequence in later movies, it remains the defining moment of the series. For now at least.

KNOW-HOW

Ready to set-jet off? Whether visiting some of the world's most popular locations or getting off the beaten path, consider these points before you screen travel.

Traveling to the real-life locations behind our favorite movies and TV shows is, for many, a dream come true—to walk in the footsteps of beloved characters, to put ourselves in the scenes we can't stop recounting. When it comes to making those dreams a reality, these tips will have you screen traveling like a pro.

Fan favorites

Big hits naturally have big fan bases. Over 100 million of us worldwide went to see *Avengers: Endgame* in the cinema, for example, and we've spent over 50 billion minutes watching *Stranger Things*. Lots of fans can only mean one thing: lots of potential screen travelers.

Once little visited, some destinations have seen a phenomenal rise in tourist numbers after appearing on-screen. Croatia's walled city of Dubrovnik, for instance, saw its tourist numbers soar in the wake of *Game of Thrones*, while the number of visitors to Skellig Michael, an island off the west coast of Ireland, rose by over 40 percent in the year after *Star Wars: The Last Jedi* was released. Such an increase in visitors causes several issues, with damage to ecosystems and added pressure on local infrastructure being just two. After its appearance in *The Beach*, Maya Bay on the island of Phi Phi Leh in Thailand received around 5,000 visitors a day—so many that the Thai authorities were forced to close the beach in 2018. Following restoration, the area has since been reopened, but with several regulations in place, including limiting visitor numbers. Other places may not have restrictions, but it's always best to check ahead.

That's not to say that we shouldn't visit such locations. Consider coming off-season, maybe, to relieve pressure on a destination. Or plan to spend longer in a particular place and see more of what it has to offer beyond the famous on-screen spots; the further your money goes, the better it is for the destination.

Into the wild

Not every movie location is a major city or a famous tourist site. In fact, some of the places that have most captivated our imaginations are off-the-beaten-path natural landscapes. New Zealand is the most obvious example; brought to life by *The Lord of the Rings* trilogy, this country bursts with beautiful spots, including Mount Sunday, the Kawarau River Canyon, and Paradise. Many such remote or natural screen locations are accessible by organized tours, but for

ON THE MAP

It's well worth downloading the SetJetters app *(www.setjetters. com)* for your adventures. This handy app contains a comprehensive list of movie locations, all plotted onto a map, meaning you can easily pinpoint the exact spot your favorite scene was filmed.

those of you who want to go it alone, prepare in the same way you would for any outdoor adventure. Ensure you have the right footwear and sensible clothing, a map and compass (cell signal for devices can vary), and tell someone where you're going and when you plan to return.

When exploring the natural world, it's also important to leave no trace. This could be as simple as taking your litter home with you, not disturbing wildlife, or keeping to paths to prevent damage to fragile flora. Always research where you can legally explore, too—in some countries, such as Scotland, the right to roam allows visitors access to most outdoor areas, providing you behave responsibly; other places, though, may have stricter rules.

Responsible set-jetting

While many places are open to screen travelers, there are certain locations we don't recommend visiting. Schools are off-limits, as are private addresses. As such, you won't find the likes of *Mean Girls* and *Clueless* in this book (both were filmed at working high schools in the US) or the private homes featured in *Breaking Bad*, *Home Alone,* or *The Goonies*. If you're visiting residential streets (and we do mention a few throughout *The Screen Traveler's Guide*), avoid lingering outside doorways and windows, and be respectful when taking photographs, particularly when homeowners display signs asking you not to.

Such consideration also goes a long way when visiting the likes of churches, temples, historical sites, and museums. Sure, these places are usually well-trodden spots, but many people will be visiting for religious or cultural reasons, so it's always best to be aware of any etiquette associated with the site and to act respectfully.

Safe travels

For some locations, there may be safety considerations to bear in mind. Due to the potential for flash floods, for instance, access to the concreted bed of the LA River is banned; don't worry, though, you can enjoy this silver screen star with a stroll along sections of its banks (the view is much better from on high, anyway). A general rule? If you're planning to visit a more offbeat movie location, always check if there are any safety issues with local information sources, such as a tourist board.

Lost locations

There are some locations that you can't visit, simply because they no longer exist. Stardust Casino, which stood in for the fictional Bazooko Circus casino in *Fear and Loathing in Las Vegas*, was demolished in 2007, while the Azure Window on Malta, a natural sea arch featured in *Game of Thrones*, collapsed during a storm in 2017. Little trace remains of Beckton Gasworks either, which appeared in Stanley Kubrick's *Full Metal Jacket*; in fact, the area it once occupied is now home to an industrial estate and two retail parks. In a nutshell, things can change fast, so always do your research before heading off.

TOP TIPS

USE PUBLIC TRANSPORTATION

While on location, try to take public transportation whenever possible. Not only will you reduce your carbon footprint, but you may also get to see a different side to your favorite on-screen destinations.

GO LOCAL ON TOURS

When searching for an organized tour of a location, try to choose a locally run company, so your money goes back into the local community.

CARRY A ZERO-WASTE KIT

Cut back on single-use plastics when screen traveling by bringing a couple of reusable items with you. Refillable water bottles and reusable coffee cups always come in handy.

GIVE BACK

Some on-screen locations offer conservation volunteering, like planting trees and monitoring wildlife. Contact National Park Service in the US or Forestry England in the UK for more information.

INDEX

Page numbers **in bold** refer to main entries.

ACKNOWLEDGMENTS

DK Eyewitness would like to thank the following people for their contributions to this project:

Jamie Andrew is a blogger and writer based in Scotland. He's contributed to *Den of Geek* for over a decade and writes a blog at *www.jamieandrew.withhands.com.* He enjoys TV shows and movies that strike at the heart of the human condition— though there's always room for both heart-warmers and barn-stormers.

Dave Bradley writes about games, TV, movies, and books, and hosts talks and panels around the world. He was editor in chief of *SFX* for a decade, and launched *Comic Heroes* and *Crime Scene.* His words appear on sites like *Pocket Gamer and Beyond Games.* When not on the road, he lives with his wife and cats near Bath.

Maine-based **Ryan Britt** is an author, journalist, and professional pop-culture critic. He is the senior entertainment editor at *Fatherly,* and has written for *Esquire, Den of Geek, Inverse, The New York Times,* and *Vulture,* among others. He is the author of the nonfiction books *Luke Skywalker Can't Read* (2015), *Phasers on Stun!* (2022), and *The Spice Must Flow* (2023), from Plume Books.

Elliot Burr is a freelance writer and marketer based in London. He can be found waxing lyrical about his favorite punk and metal records for multiple online publications. As a fan of anything surreal or explicable in cinema, his top three movies are *Mulholland Drive, Napoleon Dynamite,* and *The Cat in the Hat.*

Louis Chilton is a London-based writer and culture journalist who currently works for *The Independent*, and who has previously written for publications, including the *i* and *Little White Lies.* He is a fan of world cinema and the movies of the Coen brothers, and spends too much time rewatching *The Simpsons.*

Sarah Dobbs is a freelance writer and social media consultant. Her favorite genre is horror, but that hasn't scared her away from visiting many of the locations behind her favorite movies. She currently lives in a converted Victorian psychiatric hospital with her husband and two cats, to whom she attributes any unexplained noises or sudden chills.

Richard Edwards is a freelance writer and journalist based in Bath. He's a former editor of *SFX*, where he wrote extensively about *Star Wars, Star Trek*, superheroes, and more. Now, he's a regular contributor to a range of publications and websites including *SFX, Total Film, GamesRadar+,* and *Space.com.*

Tai Gooden is a pop culture and entertainment editor/writer, critic, and interviewer based in South Carolina. Her work can be found in such places as *Nerdist, Den of Geek, VICE,* and *The She Series Book.* When she's not working, she loves to watch and theorize about *Stranger Things, Doctor Who, Yellowjackets, The Walking Dead, The Lord of the Rings,* and all things horror.

Londoner **Rosie Knight** is a journalist and comic book writer, who now lives by the beach. You can find her work at sites like *IGN, Nerdist, The Hollywood Reporter, Esquire,* and *Den of Geek.* She is also the co-host of Crooked Media's *X-Ray Vision* podcast. Her most recent published comic work was *Godzilla Rivals Vs. Battra* with artist Oliver Ono.

Leila Latif is a writer and broadcaster. She grew up in Sudan, came-of-age in Brighton, and settled in London with her husband, two kids, a thriving sourdough starter, and a prized Blu-Ray of *Ganja & Hess.* She is contributing editor to *Total Film,* hosts *Little White Lies'* podcast, and is a regular at the BBC, *The Guardian, Sight & Sound,* and *Indiewire.*

James Macdonald is a cartographer and designer based in London. His work has been featured in books published by DK, Rough Guides, Insight, and Berlitz Guides, as well as in national papers and on TV shows. He's most likely found at a British Film Institute screening or out searching for obscure suburban locations from 1980s sci-fi series.

Librarian by day and scribbler by night, **Gem Seddon** is a Seattle-based entertainment writer with bylines at *Vulture*, *Digital Spy*, *Tech-Radar,* and *Total Film*. She loves writing about horror movies and enjoys traveling to spooky movie locales. *Alien* and *Scream* are tied as her all-time favorite movie—please don't make her choose.

Ian Haydn Smith is the editor of *1001 Movies You Must See Before You Die* and author of *A Chronology of Film*, *Well Documented,* and *The Short Story of Photography*. A curator, programmer, and broadcaster, he works regularly with the British Council, BAFTA, and the British Film Institute, as well as a number of international movie, arts, and culture festivals. In an ideal world, he would visit every location featured in this book.

Adam Smith is a UK-based movie and culture journalist who has written for the *Radio Times*, *The Telegraph*, *The Independent,* and *GQ*. He is a contributing editor for *Empire*, a member of the London Critics' Circle, and the author of *The Rough Guide to 21st Century Cinema*. He enjoys explaining, at great length and to anyone who will listen, why Leone's *Once Upon a Time In America* is better than *The Godfather*.

DK Eyewitness also thanks **David Powell** (location manager for numerous productions, including *Cruella*, *Doctor Strange,* and *The Gentlemen*), **Hayley Armstrong** (head of production services for Creative England), and **Ian Haydn Smith** for their contributions to "On Location."

Thanks also to Elspeth Beidas, Tijana Todorinovic, Rachel Laidler, Zoë Rutland, Charlie Baker, Donna-Marie Scrase, and Lucy Richards, with special mention to Robin Moul and DK's Geek Club.

References for quotations

p22 column 2, lines 22–3 (and on to p24): "Designing The Avengers: The Art of Marvel's Most Ambitious Movie," *Gizmodo* (2012).

p66 column 2, lines 1–3: "Fact scarier than fiction," *Daily Telegraph* (2007).

p68 column 1, line 4: "Scariest Film of the Year? 'Pan's Labyrinth' Director Spills His Guts," *MTV* (2006).

p80 column 2, line 3: "Paul King: What I learned writing 'Paddington,'" London Screenwriters' Festival (2020).

p96 column 2, line 10: "Steven Spielberg felt 'resentment and anger' making Schindler's List, Jurassic Park simultaneously," as reported in *Entertainment Weekly* (2018).

p123 column 1, lines 12–16: "Behind the scenes on Jordan Peele's 'Us,'" *Fandom* (2019).

p136 column 1, lines 12–13: "Peaky Blinders," Screen Yorkshire.

p170 column 2, lines 22–3: "Why Jon Favreau Chose Baby Yoda: 'We Don't Know a Lot of Details About His Species,'" *The Hollywood Reporter* (2019).

p172 column 1, lines 11–12: McBride, J., *Steven Spielberg: A Biography* (1997). New York City: Faber and Faber.

p194 column 2, lines 7–9: "This Is the Century City Skyscraper That Became a 'Leading Man' with Bruce Willis in 'Die Hard'—30 Years Later," *LA Taco* (2018).

p198 column 2, lines 1–6: "The French Connection director William Friedkin says, 'I don't think I'd make a cop film today,'" *Entertainment Weekly* (2021).

p204 column 1, line 15: "Ang Lee on 'Crouching Tiger, Hidden Dragon' 20 Years Later," *The Diplomat* (2020).

p208 column 2, line 3: "Where was Hot Fuzz filmed?," *Radio Times.com* (2022).

p213 column 2, line 13–16: "How Tom Cruise pulled off that 'Mission: Impossible 4' skyscraper climb and canceled his retirement from the blockbuster franchise," *Yahoo Entertainment* (2021).

The publisher would like to thank the following for their kind permission to reproduce their photographs:

(Key: a-above; b-below/bottom; c-center; f-far; l-left; r-right; t-top)

4Corners: Massimo Borchi 149tr, Manfred Bortoli 29bl, Susanne Kremer 152tc, Luigi Vaccarella 149cr, Chris Warren 77r
Adam Goff: 44-45
Alamy Stock Photo: Photo 12 10br, 133bl, Tono Balaguer / agefotostock 89br, Nathaniel Agueros 26cl, Jim Allan 76bl, dpa picture alliance 141cra, Granger - Historical Picture Archive 9cra, HBO / PictureLux / The Hollywood Archive 16bl, Mario Perez / HBO / The Hollywood Archive 96bl, Netflix / The Hollywood Archive 107c, PictureLux / The Hollywood Archive 12bl, World History Archive 10ca, Steve Taylor ARPS 58br, Andy Arthur 103br, United Artists 12cl, Paul Ashby 28tl, Associated Press / Fabian Bimmer 212cla, A. Astes 81bl, ATGImages 103cl, CulturalEyes - AusGS2 119tl, Jon Bilous 162bl, Stuart Black 16c, Barbara Boensch 89c, Christina Bollen 137c, Piere Bonbon 125bl, Braindead 62cl, Cezza 183c, Benjamin Ching 199cl, Werner Herzog Filmproduktion / ZDF / Collection Christohel 13cr, Collection Christophel 10bl, Walter Cicchetti 163cr, New Line Cinema 64bc, New Line Cinema 85bc, Clearview 52cr, Bruno Coelho 91cla, Sorin Colac 155cl, A7A collection 110bc, Universal Pictures / Moviestore Collection 14bl, Columbia 96cl, Chris Cooper-Smith 208bl, David Cooper 78cl, 20th Century Fox Film Corp 111bc, British Lion Film Corporation 141br, Ian Dagnall 136t, Ian G Dagnall 189c, Ian Dewar 131c, Angel Di Bilio 203br, Erwin Dimal 203cr, Sebastian Kahnert / dpa 146-147cr, Wolfgang Kumm / dpa 176tl, Mindaugas Dulinskas 42bl, David a Eastley 121tr, RossHelen editorial 124br, Chad Ehlers 202bc, Elenaphotos 13br, elephantpix 179bc, Greg Balfour Evans 110-111c, Ryan Fidrick 193cr, 20th Century Fox film 179tr, Hand Made Films 171tr, Atlaspix / 20th Century Fox 15bl, Dennis Frates 52tr, freeartist 89tc, Tony French 42ca, steven gillis 125tl, Franz Berlich / mauritius images GmbH 17cla, Prisma by Dukas Presseagentur GmbH 183cr, Steve Vidler / mauritius images GmbH 79bl, Steve Vidler / mauritius images GmbH 151br, United Archives GmbH 13bl, 14br, Ian Goodrick 55cl, Granada 57cr, Kenneth Grant 83ca, Leigh Green 17tl, De Laurentis Entertainment Group 131cr, Zoonar / u+h.eggenberger 129c, Tom Hanley 151tr, HBO 50bl, 164bc, HBO 15br, Guizhou Franck / hemis. fr 64-65, Nataliya Hora 55c, Angelo Hornak 38cr, I-Wei Huang 78tc, Hufton+Crow-View 41c, Image Professionals Gmbh / Tobias Richter 200-201c, Stefan Schurr / imageBroker 62tc, Gary Crabbe / Enlightened Images 163bc, Historica Graphica Collection / Heritage Images 9bc, Panoramic Images 86c, PSL Images 143tr, iMarGo 78bl, Everett Collection Inc 8c, Dennis Jacobsen 108c, Brian Jannsen 93cl, Jansos 142br, Jon Arnold Images Ltd / Jon Arnold 36tl, Dominic Jones 51br, Andrew Kearton 58bl, John Kellerman 151c, Yury Kirillov 122bl, Jesse Kraft 179cl, Joana Kruse 209tc, Douglas Lander 67tl, Landmark Media 190bl, Lankowsky 35bl, Jon Lauriat 36cl, Chon Kit Leong 91bl, Porridge Picture Library 55cr, Warner Bros / All Star Picture Library 12br, Jon Arnold Images Ltd 93bc, Moviestore Collection Ltd 7c, Paramount Pictures / Lucasfilm 87cr, David Lyons 113crb, Maridav 94c, Stefano Politi Markovina 68bc, Francisco Martinez 7br, Angus McComiskey